ALSO BY CHERYL RICHARDSON

Stand Up for Your Life

Life Makeovers

Take Time for Your Life

The Unmistakable
Touch of Grace

———◆———

CHERYL RICHARDSON

FREE PRESS

NEW YORK • LONDON • TORONTO • SYDNEY

*f*P

FREE PRESS
A Division of Simon & Schuster, Inc.
1230 Avenue of the Americas
New York, New York 10020

Copyright © 2005 by Cheryl Richardson

FREE PRESS and colophon are registered trademarks
of Simon & Schuster, Inc.

For information about special discounts for bulk purchases, please contact
Simon & Schuster Special Sales:
1-800-456-6798 or business@simonandschuster.com

DESIGNED BY PAUL DIPPOLITO

Manufactured in the United States of America

10 9 8 7 6 5 4 3 2 1

Library of Congress Cataloging-in-Publication Data
is available.

ISBN   0-7432-2652-6

To Michael
You are my everything.

To Marilyn
The best midwife a writer ever had.

To René,
Keep your eyes open for the spiritual change agents in your life! ♡
Cheryl

CONTENTS

ACKNOWLEDGMENTS

I am privileged and grateful to have so many very special people who support me and my work. It is with deep appreciation that I acknowledge them here.

To Marilyn Abraham, thank you for your love, unwavering encouragement, and creative collaboration. I cherish our partnership. To Max Dilley (aka BH), thank you for standing by my side on this spiritual adventure. To Daena Giardella, a master of the creative process, thank you for showing me how to use the critical voices in my head as a catalyst to write from my heart. To Kerri Richardson, thank you for your careful editing and perspective on the world of words. I love you, Sis! To Fran Massey, thank you for your thoughtful feedback and loving friendship. To Carol Look, thank you for keeping me sane with your wise counsel and keen intuition. And a heartfelt thanks to Jerry Thomas for leading me to a deeper and richer relationship with God.

A big thanks to the dear friends and colleagues who inspire, encourage, and enlighten me: Chris Barnes, Jonathan Berg, Ginger Burr, Andrew Carroll, Alan Clements, Stephen Cluney, Lama Surya Das, Katy Davis, Joseph Denucci, Deirdre DiDonna, Aryn Ekstedt, Rich and Kathy Fettke, Debbie Ford, Peter Girouard, Connie Kelley, Tom Kenison, Bruce Kohl (mfgm), Sandy MacGregor, Kelly O'Brien, Niravi Payne, Chris Rauchnot, Terry Real, Pat Rogers, Wren

Ross, SARK, Steve Shull, Stephen Simon, Debbie Stier, Judy Tache, Susan Taylor, David Thorne, Wyatt Webb, and Ellen Wingard. I love and appreciate you all very much.

A special thanks to the women in my dialogue group: Nanna Aida Svendsen, Helen Gitkind (my shell sister), Pat Adler, and Ro Gordon. Thank you to the kind people at Miraval Life In Balance, Diane Baxter and the gals at Nutcracker Bakery, Joyce at Angie's, and to Alanis, for the musical inspiration that fueled my writing.

I am very fortunate to have an outstanding group of people who provide me and my online community with direction and support. First and foremost is my personal assistant, Jan Silva, whose commitment, sense of humor, and generous spirit make life so much better for me and for thousands of people around the world. Thank you, Super Jan! Nancy Levin, whose energy and enthusiasm make traveling and teaching a joy—thank you for your devotion to this work and for being such a dear friend. Thank you to Linda Waraska for making sure everyone gets what they need (including me!). Many thanks to Laura Franklin, Brett Rabideau, and Mogenns Gilmour for supporting our web community; to Robin Gillette for keeping the books; and to Barry Crites and Ginger Burr for making hair and makeup fun. I love you all.

My agent, Amanda Urban, is top-notch. Thank you for taking such good care of me. Thanks also to John DeLaney, Karen Kenyon, Margaret Halton, Betsy Robbins, Elizabeth Iveson, and all the folks at ICM who support me and my work.

A big thank you to my publishing team: Dominick Anfuso, who encouraged me to write my truth; Martha

Levin, whose thoughtfulness kept me on track; Carisa Hays, who does an outstanding job with publicity; and to Michele Jacobs, Suzanne Donahue, Wylie O'Sullivan, Clare Wulker, Ellen Raspitha, Edith Lewis, and everyone at Free Press. I appreciate you all!

A heartfelt thank you to Oprah for the powerful influence you continue to have on my life.

Many thanks to Ania O'Connor for your hands and heart, as well as to Annie Twiss and Christine Misiano-Cornelisse. Thanks also to Joyce Trout for offering your home as a writing retreat. And a big thank you to Laine Jones, Bernie Christopher, and Paul Miller for your commitment to building our dream.

I am informed and inspired by my clients and the thousands of people in our Life Makeover Community who have contributed so much to this book. The influence of every conversation, coaching call, or e-mail can be found in these pages. A special thank you to the retreat/telegathering gang for their feedback, great ideas, and beautiful stories, and to the gals at the barn who helped set this book on the right course.

Thank you to my family for your unconditional love and support—Mom, Dad, Steven, Janice, Donna, Tom, Lisa, Walter, Shelly, Mark, Robert, Karen, Kerri, Missy, and my in-laws Pat and Curt Gerrish. I love you all very much.

To the team who supports my company—Barry Coscia, Tom Godino, and Steven Richardson—thank you all for your friendship and thoughtful advice. And a special thank you to my attorney, Mark Lawless, for your skill, sense of humor, and professional insight. I feel so grateful to have you in my life.

Thanks to the gang at Hay House, in particular Reid Tracy, for your friendship and guidance. Many thanks to my UK team at Transworld Publishers, including Brenda Kimber, Larry Finlay, Teria Boley, Helen Edwards, and everyone who takes care of my books across the pond.

Thank you to a team of great coaches—Nancy Baker, Sharon Day, and Sally McCue—for taking such good care of the Life Makeover Community while I worked on this book, and to all the professional coaches and folks at the International Coach Federation.

And to my husband, Michael, whose hard work, editing, influence, and love can be found on every page of this book: How did a woman get so lucky to have so much in one man? I love you infinity × infinity.

And finally and most important—to God, the Divine force that guides and supports my life.

The Unmistakable
Touch of Grace

INTRODUCTION

———◆———

My Gift to You

ONE DECISION, MADE ALMOST twenty years ago, altered the course of my life and brought us here together in this moment. Since then I've come to believe that my life is guided by a powerful Divine force, and when I choose to align myself with this energy, the best and most advantageous path unfolds before me.

I've also learned that there are no coincidences. Every event we experience and every person we meet has intentionally been put in our path to help raise our level of consciousness. When we awaken to this fundamental truth, life becomes a true adventure, a spiritual adventure. The person who smiles at you while you're walking down the street is no longer a stranger. The phone call from an old friend who crossed your mind the day before is no longer a surprise. And the failed relationship that left you brokenhearted is no longer a source of bitterness and pain. Instead it's seen as a blessing in disguise, a gift that makes you stronger, more conscious, and ultimately, more alive.

Over time, as you come to understand these events for what they really are, you recognize that a benevolent force of energy has been available to guide and direct your life all along. I call this energy "the unmistakable touch of grace."

DEFINING GRACE

Grace comes from the Latin word *gratia,* meaning favor, charm, or thanks. Spiritual traditions from around the world each share a similar understanding of this word. For example, in Sanskrit, grace is akin to the word *grnati,* which means He praises, and to call or invoke. In Christian terms, grace is defined as the infinite love, mercy, favor, and goodwill shown by God to humankind. In Judaism, the concept of grace is expressed by the Hebrew word *hesed,* meaning mercy, or loving-kindness. Grace is seen as a creative force—an act of exceptional kindness and goodness. And my friend, Lama Surya Das, author of *Awakening the Buddha Within,* and a leading Buddhist teacher, says, "Grace is the 'isness' of life. It's the recognition that everything is connected and sacred. The more in touch we are with this natural abundance of life, the less we need."

To me, grace is a kind of spiritual intelligence, a form of energy that comes from the Divine Source. This energy is available to each and every one of us at any moment. When we connect with and trust this Higher Power and follow its lead, we step into alignment with a larger vision for our lives. We wake up and suddenly become aware of signs, symbols, and messages that lead us to our highest good.

How do you arrive at a place where you view your life from this perspective? By opening your eyes and your heart to a new way of looking at yourself and the world. One decision is all it takes to get started. From there, your life can change in ways you never could have imagined.

Many people begin this journey when faced with a life crisis or challenge that inspires them to begin making different choices. I've seen it time and again in my career as a coach. "Life change" has been the focus of my work for the last eighteen years. I've taught self-management techniques, offered strategies to eliminate procrastination and energy drains, and preached the gospel of self-care from one end of the country to the other. Along the way I've helped people to see the meaning and purpose behind what appear to be random, everyday events that are, in fact, signposts directing them to a new and better life.

My first two books were primarily focused on helping readers to manage their external lives—finances, relationships, or busy schedules. My most recent book, *Stand Up for Your Life,* shifted gears and challenged readers to turn inward to develop the qualities of character that would allow them to live a more soul-directed life. My writing and teaching have always been a direct result of my own experience. For example, I wrote my first book, *Take Time for Your Life,* because I didn't have one. And, as I became better able to honor my top priorities, I shared what I learned with others.

FINDING THE RIGHT DIRECTION

As I considered the topic for this book, I felt conflicted. My head told me to continue to write about tangible topics like overcoming procrastination or improving financial health—topics that I knew were important to my readers' lives. Yet, as I began to develop these ideas on paper, I quickly discovered that my heart wasn't in it. I felt moved to write from a deeper, more personal place about my emergence from an unconscious life and my evolving spiritual journey. I wanted to share what I had learned about the myths of success and the reality of what I believe it takes to lead a meaningful life. I worked on outlines for two different books, and then, faced with a deadline, I did what I often do when I need clarity and inspiration—I went to the beach.

I am blessed to have six miles of federally protected shoreline on an island near my home. The coastline stretches out farther than the eye can see, and I can get lost for hours in the beauty of the open ocean. Once there, I walked along the water's edge and began to pray out loud. "Dear God, I have to make a decision about my next book and I don't know what to do. I'm tired of struggling so I'm surrendering it all to you. Please allow me to be open to seeing the right choice." Then, I continued my walk.

Sometime later the phrase "the unmistakable touch of grace" popped into my head. "Hmm," I thought, "what a beautiful expression." As I slowly made my way down the beach I started to think about how grace has influenced my life.

Since my late twenties, I started noticing unusual occurrences, what some would call coincidences, that provided me with guidance and direction when I felt lost or unsure of myself. I remember one incident early in my career as a professional speaker, when I felt stuck and questioned whether I should continue. I had been looking for a speaker's bureau to represent me and was having trouble finding one. The pressure of trying to make it work was frustrating and one morning, as I was ready to throw in the towel, my phone rang. When I picked it up and said hello, I heard a woman's voice say, "Faith?" "Excuse me?" I replied. "Who are you looking for?" "Faith Richardson," she answered, and a few seconds later the phone went dead. I stood in my living room staring at the receiver in my hand. A smile slowly crossed my face as I realized I had my answer. I needed to trust myself and hang in there. I needed to have faith.

As I thought more about the unmistakable touch of grace during my walk, I could also see that writing about this topic would address the epidemic of fear, anxiety, and disconnectedness I've found in audiences while speaking throughout the country. As I talk to people about their lives, I often see a distant, almost vacant look in their eyes—a look that says "I'm so busy trying to *survive* my life that I have no soul left to live it." The events of September 11, and the chaos in the Middle East, along with the overwhelming amount of information and stimuli that assault us on a daily basis, have caused our anxiety levels to soar. Living on the edge of uncertainty has made fight or flight our standard operating mode.

As technology continues to give people more ways to intrude on our time, we end up retreating from the world in an attempt to shelter ourselves from a busy, chaotic life. Clients often tell me that they spend so much time on the phone or computer communicating with people at work that they no longer have the energy or desire to talk with their friends or family when they get home. As a result, our most soul-nourishing relationships start to deteriorate and we end up feeling lonely and isolated. We can try to fill the hollowness inside with everything from the latest reality TV show, to overspending, or the restless pursuit of a purposeful career, only to be disappointed when the emptiness remains. It's no wonder most of us feel as though something essential is missing from our lives. There is. We are starved for a connection to the sacred dimension of life.

I understand the dilemma. I feel privileged to have experienced the kind of success that most people only dream of. I've written books that have made the *New York Times* bestseller list, built a large online community that brings together thousands of people from around the world, and had the amazing opportunity to lead a series on "The Oprah Winfrey Show." As my career took off and my schedule filled up, I got seduced by my own busy life and lost sight of my spiritual center. I became more focused on leaping the next highest bar. One bestseller wasn't enough. There had to be another. As soon as I accomplished an important goal, I automatically moved on to the next, never allowing myself an opportunity to enjoy the fruits of my hard work. Enough was never enough and even when I knew better, it still wasn't enough. These accomplishments (and the life lessons that ensued) gave me the rare opportunity to know for sure that no amount of money, popularity, or success can give us the happiness and peace we all long for. This comes from the daily rituals and practices that keep us connected to our spiritual core.

As someone who has dedicated her life to helping people honor their values and most treasured priorities, it's clear to me the answer to living a genuine, soul-directed life is not just about practicing time management techniques or self-care strategies. While these tools are important, as long as we look for solutions in the outer world to calm our fears and anxieties, or to alleviate our loneliness, we'll always be disappointed. Instead, we need to go deeper. We must embrace what great spiritual teachers have known all along—freedom from suffering and true happiness are found in the connection we share with a power greater than us all.

I left the beach that day with a greater sense of clarity and feeling more excited about the direction I wanted this book to take. So I made a decision to sit with the phrase, "the unmistakable touch of grace," to see what happened.

Later that night while lying in bed, I continued to reflect on my experience and relationship with grace. I truly believe that more than anything else, my commitment to live a spiritually based life has been the source of my success. The more I surrender my will to the Divine, the less I've had to worry about how to achieve anything. Instead, the path finds me. Grace leads me to the exact events and experiences I need at exactly the right time.

There have been striking examples of this throughout my life. Sometimes the messages were like whispers—an unexpected e-mail with a helpful invitation, or a call from a colleague at the exact moment I needed support. Other times, they were like a loud roar commanding my attention. Let me give you an example of what I mean.

Several years ago, my friend Max and I were having a conversation during a sunset walk along the beach. I had just ended a five-year relationship and felt conflicted about my decision. Deep in my heart I knew separating was the right choice, yet I kept feeling pulled to call my former partner to give it one more try. Max, being the good friend that she is, encouraged me to stay true to myself. She suggested that I focus on my own self-care and the new emerging chapter of my life.

Like so many of us who go through a tough life transition, I felt pulled in two directions. In my heart I knew that I needed to hold still and stay strong, but my head screamed, "Call him!" I felt as though I was caught in an emotional battle of wills, struggling to keep the peace between two feuding factions.

As Max and I continued our conversation, I said that I needed a sign—some kind of divine confirmation to help me make the right choice. Just then, I looked up and saw a man running toward us. He was striking; muscular and tanned, with piercing blue eyes. When he passed us, Max and I looked at each other and smiled, acknowledging his powerful energy. We continued our walk and eventually headed for the car.

Arriving at the parking lot, we sat down to put on our shoes. Taking one more look out over the ocean, I once again saw the same man running back down the beach. As my eyes followed him, he suddenly stopped, bent down and started to scratch something in the sand with his finger. After a few moments he finished and continued on his way. Max and I immediately ran to see what he had written.

When we arrived at the water's edge we found the words MENTAL TOUGHNESS scrawled in the sand. Stunned, I stood looking at the words, amazed at how appropriate and timely they were for me. When I glanced up to find the angel who had delivered this message, he was nowhere in sight. Instantly I felt a sense of relief and reassurance. I knew I had my answer—hold still and stay strong.

Stories like this are powerful examples of grace in action. They give us comfort and a sense of direction. Sometimes we see the influence of grace in hindsight when we step back and view our lives from a higher perspective. When I look back at my early years in high school, I can see that the two teachers who fueled my passion for reading set the stage for my future career as a writer. Or, the difficulties I faced in my relationships with men were exactly what I needed to build the solid core of self-esteem and inner strength that I would rely on to face the challenges of life. Even the most agonizing experiences of all—the death of a loved one and the diagnosis of a serious illness, turned out to be blessings; pivotal events that dramatically altered the way I live my life today.

CONDUCTING MY OWN EXPERIMENT

The morning after the phrase "the unmistakable touch of grace" first came to me, I woke feeling energized and excited. If I was going to write about grace, I wanted to engage this energy and allow it to guide my next steps. I made a decision to keep that phrase in my mind and watch for what showed up in my life. Almost immediately I began to see the signs.

That afternoon a friend called, excited to share a story of what she called synchronicity. Emma was a new writer who'd been invited to submit an article to her local newspaper. Even though she'd done a terrific job with her first draft, she kept procrastinating about finishing it up and sending it to her editor. After admitting her hesitation, Emma revealed that, like most new writers, she was afraid of having her article rejected. Each time she got close to hitting the send button on her e-mail, she'd freeze and back away.

Two days later, Emma attended a professional women's luncheon. When introductions were being made around the table, Emma was shocked to discover that the assistant editor of the newspaper was sitting next to her. During the meal, the two women struck up a conversation and Emma shared her dilemma about the article. The editor, sympathetic to the anxiety that new writers experience, offered to look at the article, off the record, and suggest changes if necessary. Her support was all Emma needed. When she arrived home after the luncheon, she immediately sent the article to the editor. Three weeks later, she was a published writer.

Was it merely a coincidence that Emma was seated next to this editor? Could be. But after the many times I've witnessed these kinds of events, both in my life and in the lives of others, I no longer believe this to be the case. Instead, I see them as examples of how recognizing and acting on the effects of grace leads us in the best direction for our lives.

The signs continued. Later that week while driving to the cleaners to pick up a dress for an anniversary celebration with my husband, Michael, I noticed the beautiful peonies that were blooming in our neighborhood. These flowers had been a special part of our wedding day and I made a mental note to pick some up on my way home. When I finished my errands, I pulled in the driveway, only to realize that I had forgotten to get the flowers. Feeling pressed for time, I decided to let it go. I parked the car, gathered my bags, and headed for the front door.

Just then my neighbor, Gail, arrived with a gorgeous bunch of pink and white peonies in her arms. "Hey Cheryl," she said, "I just finished cutting these from my garden and wondered if you might like some." I smiled, feeling strongly that, once again, I was touched by the hand of grace. To me, it was one more sign that I was on the right track with the book.

There were plenty of other signs telling me that I needed to write about grace. A favorite magazine arrived with a cover story entitled "Living a Life of Grace." After discussing the idea of grace with a member of my staff, she called later that day to say that grace had been the topic of her yoga class. And of course, it seemed that every time I got in my car to drive somewhere a Grace Happens bumper sticker was staring me in the face.

The final message came two days later after a speaking engagement in Manhattan. While there, I had dinner with a friend who introduced me to a woman named Michele. Michele was an intuitive consultant and writer. During our conversation, she suggested that I take a look at her website to learn more about her work. As I jotted down her address, Michele also said, "Be sure to check out 'word magic.' It's an area that visitors seem to love." I included word magic in my notes and continued our conversation.

The next day, as I sat in my office going through the notes from my trip, I came across Michele's information. I logged on to her website and clicked on the phrase, *word magic.* I discovered that it was a prophetic game whereby the visitor holds a question in mind while several colored spheres circle around the page to the sound of calming music. Then, when ready, the visitor clicks on a sphere to reveal a word that represents the answer.

As I watched the spheres on the screen I focused on my question: "Which topic do I need to write about in my next book?" Then, I stopped for a moment, closed my eyes and pictured the spheres. When I opened my eyes I was immediately drawn to a lavender colored one, and, without hesitation, clicked on it and waited to see what happened. I saw the word *grace* appear and float slowly toward me on the screen. I felt chills run through my body; I could hardly believe what I was seeing.

Being a skeptic by nature, I immediately called Michele. Like so many of us who get Divine signs, I doubted my experience and wanted to know what the odds were of seeing the word *grace.* I was convinced that each of the eight spheres represented one word and I had a one out of eight chance of choosing it—odds that, to me, weren't very impressive. As luck would have it, Michele immediately picked up the phone. She was shocked to hear my voice on the other end. "I was just sending you an e-mail." Another coincidence?

When I asked Michele about the game, she told me that there were more than seventy-five words available to be assigned to a sphere at any given moment. And, since the words were assigned at random with each visit to her site, the chances of choosing the sphere that represented grace was pretty slim. Several weeks later my friend Ed, a mathematics professor, confirmed this when he informed me that the odds of seeing that word appear were more than a million to one.

Some might say that these events were simply the result of focusing my attention on the topic of grace. And, in the past, I would have thought so too. But, experience has taught me that these examples are not just the result of wishful thinking. They are a response from a Divine Source that guides and directs my life.

Science tells us that the universe vibrates with the same force of energy that created it in the first place; the same energy that created you and me. As we raise our level of consciousness and learn to work in partnership with this Divine energy, it provides a feedback loop of sorts, a way of communicating with us that takes the form of signs. *The more awake or conscious we are, the better able we are to see these signs for what they really are—unmistakable evidence of how grace shapes our lives.*

My friend Peter, a recovering alcoholic, said it well: "Before I got sober, I couldn't see a Divine sign if it hit me in the face. I was living under the influence, too unconscious to recognize that a power greater than myself was attempting to offer the guidance and support I needed to change my life. When I finally woke up and got into recovery, things changed dramatically. Suddenly I could see the gifts of grace everywhere. They were constant reminders that I was not alone and that as long as I stayed sober and paid attention, I'd be guided to the life I was meant to live."

I've watched this same kind of thing happen in my work with clients. Regardless of their beliefs or spiritual orientation, once clients made the decision to wake up, they could see and experience grace. For example, I'd watch the president of a company cut back on his hours at work to spend more time with his family, only to have his sales *increase*. Or, conversely I'd see a stay-at-home mom with special artistic talent decide to bring her paintings to a gallery where an influential owner would steer her to great success.

Over time, as I watched what happened, one thing became quite clear—grace was unmerited. People didn't need to work hard to earn it, feel worthy enough to deserve it, or surrender their needs to receive it. The gift of grace had been available all along. They just needed to be awake enough to see it. Then, from this more conscious perspective, they would engage this power as they faced the truth about what wasn't working in their lives and began making changes. Doors would open, resources would appear, and a veil of uncertainty would lift, revealing their next step. Seeing evidence of grace allowed them to trust that there was a higher purpose for their lives, and this fueled a desire for a more conscious relationship with this Divine, creative force.

Some clients called this force God; others called it Providence, the Universe, or Spirit. There were some who had no name at all. They had lost touch with a spiritual way of life or had experienced a crisis of faith, when they felt angry with God or disconnected altogether. As a result, they needed to redefine their relationship with a Higher Power. I had been through this process myself. For years I felt uncomfortable with the word *God* because of the fear-based, parental relationship I had been encouraged to form during my early religious training. It wasn't until years later, when I made a conscious decision to combine the comforting, religious rituals of my youth with the spiritual values and practices I developed as an adult, that I would establish a new relationship with God. Although I now feel comfortable using the word *God,* I often use the word *Divine* when working with clients, in an effort to be respectful of their beliefs. Based on what I saw happening around me, it was clear that grace was operating in the lives of the people I worked with, regardless of their religious orientation.

I began to understand the significance of the phrase "the unmistakable touch of grace," and I was starting to believe more strongly that my prayer on the beach had pointed me in the right direction. Once I decided to move forward, I went back through my life looking for how my own relationship with grace had evolved over time. I read through twenty-five years worth of journals, and when I was finished, spoke with friends, clients, and members of my online community about their experiences with grace. As I sorted through this information, I wanted to find a way to help people open more fully to the presence of grace in their lives. This book is the result of that journey.

THE PROMISE

By embarking on this adventure you'll awaken to the presence of grace in your own life and sometimes, the lives of others. Whether you already feel a connection to a Higher Power or not, pretty soon you'll find that your anxiety, fear, or uncertainty about the future will gradually be replaced with the comfort and security of knowing:

- *You are not alone.* There is a powerful, supportive energy guiding your life and it always has your best interest at heart. When you call upon it for guidance and support, it will respond. Spiritual signposts will be put in your path to guide you to your highest good. Follow them!

- *You have a higher purpose for your life.* The more you surrender to Divine will and allow grace to lead, the more you'll find that the right doors open to support you in fulfilling your life's purpose. You'll learn to recognize and respond to them. Walk through those doors with courage and faith.

- *You have what it takes to face any life challenge.* As a human being you will experience loss, disappointment, failure, and fear. But you don't have to suffer. As a matter of fact, your most challenging life circumstance may turn out to be your greatest blessing. Your reliance on the power of grace will give you the faith and spiritual fortitude to face life's ups and downs with confidence and poise.

- *You are a student in the school of life.* As you view your life from a higher, more spiritual perspective, you'll begin to see that everything happens for a reason. Every event, experience, and person you encounter is intended to support your soul development. Take advantage of these opportunities.

- *You have the peace and happiness you desire already within you.* When you deepen your connection to the Divine by balancing activity with silence, you'll discover the true source of all joy and happiness. You'll experience a heightened sensitivity to beauty, deep inner peace, and a profound feeling of connectedness to all living things. Enjoy these gifts.

The journey you're about to take is exciting and full of promise. As you read through each chapter, allow yourself to drink in the inspiration of the stories first, without worrying about having to do anything. Stories themselves are a powerful source of grace. They give us insight and provide us with inspiration that shifts our thinking or way of being in the world.

Once you've finished reading a chapter, you'll be ready to conduct the experiment.

THE EXPERIMENTS

At the end of each chapter I've included an experiment designed to help you recognize and use the power of grace in your own life. Think of yourself as a spiritual scientist, ready to explore new territories that will alter your view of the world forever. You may also want to assemble your own team of scientists. Invite one or more people to work through this book with you. While you can conduct these experiments on your own, you'll dramatically increase your ability to see the influence of grace in *your* life by witnessing its effects on others. If you're unable to find someone, don't worry. We've made it easy for you to locate like-minded people *in your community,* by using our free global database of Life Makeover Groups on our website at www.cheryl-richardson.com. There you'll find all the tools and resources you need to find or start a group in your hometown. As I write this book, more than four thousand groups are already in action around the world.

THE RESOURCE SECTIONS

At the end of each experiment I've included a list of resources to help further your spiritual exploration. These books, websites, and other programs have been helpful during the various stages of my journey. They provide a variety of perspectives and teachings. And, while some may contain information or opinions that differ from your own, I encourage you to keep an open mind. The influence of grace is often found in unexpected places.

This book is filled with stories of how grace has touched my life and the lives of clients, friends, and members of our online community. While some stories may seem unbelievable, all of them are true (some names and details have been changed). It is my prayer that this book serve as inspiration and motivation to open you more fully to your own divinity and the sacred dimension of life. At a time when so many of us feel hopeless and powerless to change the troubled world in which we live, it's important to remember that there is a Divine power far greater than anything else that exists on the planet—a power that resides within each of us. When we learn to align our own Divine nature with the ultimate Creative Source, miracles happen. As Ramakrishna said, "The winds of grace are always blowing, but you have to raise the sail." This book is my gift to you in the hopes that it will help you to do just that.

EXPERIMENT: FINDING GRACE

The first experiment is designed to help you become more aware of the presence of grace. There are five parts to this experiment:

1. Start a grace journal. Find a journal or notebook that's easy to use for the experiments throughout this book.

2. On the first page of your journal, write the following:

   I am open and receptive to the power of grace in my life now. I ask to be shown clear examples of how this energy is operating in my life.

3. Now, declare *out loud* that you are open to the influence of grace. As silly as this may sound, it's important to get in the habit of consciously working with this energy. Try it right now. Repeat the following statement:

   I am open and receptive to the power of grace in my life now. I ask to be shown clear examples of how this energy is operating in my life.

   Develop a ritual of writing this statement in your journal every morning and night, and when you do, repeat it out loud. (If you really want to accelerate the process, repeat it at random times throughout the day).

4. Begin to focus on the concept of grace. Notice what shows up in *your* life and write about it in your journal. Does the word come up in conversations? Do you find it in a magazine article, or on bumper stickers? Start to keep track of the signs of grace that are already in your life.

5. Finally, sometimes we experience grace in how we relate to the stories of others. As you read through each chapter, pay close attention to the reactions you have to the stories you read. Does one push your buttons, move you to tears, make you angry, or cause you to daydream?

Mark the stories and write about any insights, similarities, or reactions in your journal.

Resources

BOOKS

Awakening the Buddha Within: Eight Steps to Enlightenment by Lama Surya Das (Broadway Books, 2004)

> *This book provides a great introduction to Buddhism by exploring the ancient teachings in a modern-day voice.*

Everyday Grace: Having Hope, Finding Forgiveness, and Making Miracles by Marianne Williamson (Riverhead Books, 2002)

> *A beautiful book about harnessing the mystical power within so we can change ourselves and the world.*

Roadsigns: Navigating Your Path to Spiritual Happiness by Philip Goldberg, Ph.D. (Rodale, 2003)

> *This book provides a realistic look at the twists and turns of the spiritual journey and provides wise, common-sense advice on making life choices.*

To Life: A Celebration of Jewish Being and Thinking by Harold S. Kushner (Warner Books, 1994)

> *Kushner discusses the essence of Judaism in simple and clear language, touching upon the meaning of Jewish customs and ceremonies, and the purpose of prayer.*

What's So Amazing About Grace? by Philip Yancey (Zondervan, 1997)

> *A Christian perspective on the meaning of grace told through stories and examples from everyday life.*

WEBSITES

www.beliefnet.org

> *A nondenominational website dedicated to providing a variety of information, spiritual tools, and inspiration.*

www.cherylrichardson.com

> *Use our website to find like-minded friends in your hometown.*

www.innerworldmedia.com

> *To try word magic for yourself, check out Michele Bernhardt's website.*

1

WHEN GRACE KNOCKS

THERE IS A MOMENT IN LIFE when we make a choice that changes us forever. This moment marks a turning point, a threshold of sorts, when we realize that the life we're living is not a true reflection of who we really are. For some, the choice comes as a result of a dramatic event like the sudden loss of a job, the diagnosis of a life-threatening illness, or the death of someone we love. For others, it's the result of dealing with difficult life situations like financial hardship or the long, slow end of a marriage. And sometimes this decision is driven by something less profound— you simply wake up one morning and decide that it's time for a change. You're no longer willing to live the way you've been living.

My moment came in my mid-twenties. At the time, I was engaged to a man who shared my somewhat reckless lifestyle. We worked routine jobs from 9 to 5, spent evenings at home in front of the TV, and looked forward to weekend social events where the alcohol flowed freely. If you had asked me then what I wanted out of life, I would have told you that my only desire was to be happy. I wanted to live a hassle-free life without any conflict or stress. Like many women my age, my primary focus was my relationship. I made a career out of being in love.

One Saturday night, while vacationing with some friends on Cape Cod, a group of us decided to go dancing. After a couple of hours, I went to a corner booth at the back of the club, and ordered another drink. I watched the scene. The room was smoky and people were yelling to one another over the loud music. One of my girlfriends who had had a bit too much to drink was dancing by herself in the middle of the room. At first, this all seemed normal, like any other night in a club. But a few minutes later I had a strange experience.

Amidst the loud noise and frenzy of activity, I suddenly felt as though I had stepped outside of my body and was able to view my surroundings from a more removed and objective perspective. As I witnessed the antics of my drunken friends, a voice inside me clearly said: "Cheryl, what are you doing? You don't belong here. You're meant to do so much more with your life. Wake up!"

Struck by the clarity of my thoughts (and the strangeness of my experience), I sat back, suddenly feeling anxious and uncomfortable. Sure there were times when I questioned my drinking or whether or not I belonged in this relationship, but I'd eventually ignore the little voice in my head and go back to sleep, settling into a warm state of denial that felt safe and familiar. But this time was different. In that one moment, the little voice inside me became too loud to ignore. Although I didn't understand why, there was something about the strength and clarity of its message that snapped me to my senses, and suddenly I couldn't pretend anymore. Later I would come to understand that this incident marked a turning point in my life: *Grace had knocked on my door.*

———◆———

My friend Alice would tell you that her awakening was triggered by a series of panic attacks that left her feeling terrified and afraid to leave her home. Alice's body had been trying to get her attention for quite some time. Not only did she suffer from migraine headaches and psoriasis, she was also waking up in the middle of the night with what she called fright episodes—bouts of obsessive worrying that kept her up for hours at a time.

Alice was a sales manager for a large company where she was in charge of more than thirty-five people. Throughout the day she often received over one hundred e-mails and more than fifty voice mail messages. She rarely left the office before 9 PM, and on weekends, spent much of her time playing catch up on her laptop. And if she weren't under enough stress, Alice discovered a message on her home computer that led her to believe her husband might be having an affair. But, rather than confront him about it, Alice told herself that she was being overly sensitive and paranoid. Instead, she threw herself further into her work.

One month after finding the suspicious e-mail, Alice began to have panic attacks—periods of intense anxiety that seemed to come out of the blue. Her first attack occurred while driving home from work. Scared that she was having a heart attack, she immediately drove herself to the emergency room of a nearby hospital. The examination showed nothing serious, and the doctor suggested that Alice take a few days off to relax. But, Alice ignored his advice and over the next few weeks continued to experience periods of high anxiety. She was convinced that she just needed more sleep.

One afternoon, in the middle of a meeting with an important client, Alice had another attack. She suddenly felt her chest tighten and her palms begin to sweat. Unable to ignore her symptoms, she excused herself from the meeting and had her assistant drive her to the hospital. This trip to the hospital finally sent her over the edge and forced her to wake up.

Lying in the ER on a gurney, surrounded by a flimsy curtain, Alice cried uncontrollably. She was terrified of what was happening to her body. Although her blood pressure and heart rate were elevated, the tests performed by the medical staff showed no signs of a serious problem. This time it was clear that Alice was having a panic attack.

That day grace blessed Alice in the form of a loving nurse who held her hand and comforted her as she sobbed out her pain. She talked about the insanity at work and her fear that her husband was having an affair. While listening to her story, the nurse gently stroked Alice's hair reassuring her that everything would be all right. After what seemed like hours, Alice finally felt herself calming down. The nurse, who had also experienced panic attacks, gently recommended the name of a therapist who specialized in treating anxiety disorders. Alice took the number and vowed to call as soon as she got home.

Looking back, Alice realized that her experience of grace occurred that afternoon in the emergency room. Feeling out of control and frightened, she was forced to face the truth about her health and the cause of her stress. Things were falling apart at home and she was clearly overworked. The anxiety that she experienced ended up being her saving grace and seeing a therapist set in motion the healing Alice so desperately needed. She began the long, slow process of waking up from the unconscious lifestyle she had grown accustomed to by confronting her work addiction and the reality of her failing marriage. Alice finally found within herself the willingness she needed to face the truth.

What area of your life feels out of control? How might this situation become *your* saving grace? Many of us have learned to live in a comfortable state of denial about what isn't working in our lives. We tolerate high levels of stress at work, take important relationships for granted, put our health needs on hold, or continue to overspend in spite of the anxiety we feel about our mounting debt. We get so caught up in the details of living that our busyness becomes a convenient diversion from the pesky inner voice that begs us to listen up. Here's the irony: listening to the little voice will set you free. When you finally face the truth about how you feel and begin to make even small changes, you slowly emerge from the protective cocoon of denial and allow grace to lead the way.

FACING THE TRUTH

The morning after my wake-up call in the nightclub, I was hung over and groggy. I wanted to ignore what happened the night before, but I couldn't deny the fact that my life was spinning out of control. I had to be honest. I wasn't happy. I was living in a chronic state of shame, knowing that I was settling for much less than I deserved. I was abusing my body, drinking too much, and at times, even using drugs. Part of me knew I was taking too many risks, but it seemed I had no other choice. Looking back, I can see that my feelings of unworthiness were at the root of my self-sabotage.

In the days and weeks that followed, I felt both fear and excitement as I took stock of what wasn't working in my life. My relationship with my fiancé was in jeopardy. I hated my job. My closest friends were heavy drinkers, and my body was in tough shape. The more I admitted the truth, the more frightened I became. I was starting to see how bad things really were and I felt stuck. At the time, I hadn't a clue about how to change my life. So I prayed for the courage and wherewithal to do what needed to be done. This was right about the point when things began to unravel.

My relationship with my fiancé was fraught with deception and lies. Rather than confront him about his drinking, I was dancing around it, in part, by doing my best to keep pace. As I looked closely at my relationship history, it was obvious that I kept choosing partners who were emotionally unavailable, abusive, or self-absorbed. Although my girlfriends and I often complained about how few good men there were out there, I never stopped to consider the role I played in attracting them into my life. I was starting to face reality—there wasn't a lack of good men. I was making bad choices.

My fiancé was often kind and supportive, yet he was more interested in drinking with his friends than dealing with the real issues in our relationship. As I started to see and acknowledge how much my life had spun out of control, I talked about how I thought we could make things better. I suggested that we limit our social engagements, cut back on our drinking, and make a more conscious effort to improve our communication. But, while he listened attentively and agreed that things needed to change, he would eventually go right back to doing what he had always done. In the end, I had to face the fact that I couldn't change him. He had a right to make his own choices.

AN UNEXPECTED WAKE-UP CALL

When my client Ned had his wake-up call, he chose to pay attention. Ned was in his early fifties and worked as a manufacturing engineer for a semiconductor distributor. He had been with his company for more than fifteen years and loved his job. He was well respected in his division, had a few coworkers that he occasionally socialized with, and for the most part, enjoyed working for his boss. But, during the economic downturn of 2002, his company went through a restructuring process. One afternoon, without any warning at all, Ned was called into his boss's office and told that his position had been eliminated. His boss explained that while the company would provide him with an outplacement package to help him update his job search skills, he needed to clean out his desk and leave the building by the end of the day.

It's a practice for some companies to ask employees to leave the premises immediately after being told that they've been laid off. Stories of corporate sabotage make it a necessary evil in the minds of executives who are charged with protecting company assets. But it's a humiliating and degrading practice. As someone who has counseled employees immediately after they received this kind of news, I know all too well how demoralizing it can be. And, as painful as it often is, I've also seen people use it as a vehicle to make critical, life-altering decisions. And that's exactly what Ned did.

On the afternoon that Ned was let go, he left his boss's office feeling shocked and numb. He found himself thinking about his family, his coworkers, and his financial future. What would he tell his wife? How could he possibly say goodbye to everyone in only a few short hours? What would he say to them? Soon his shock and disbelief turned into anger, and by the time he arrived home, he was enraged. When his wife met him at the door he proceeded to complain about being "betrayed by his boss and his company." As Ned became increasingly agitated, his wife recommended that he talk to a professional about how he felt. This only made Ned even more upset, so much so, that he lost control and put his fist through the kitchen wall.

The loss of a job, particularly for a man who has dedicated his life to a company and who has become so identified with his work, can wreak havoc on a marriage. Typically, both partners are forced to confront a lot of challenging issues. For example, Ned was dealing with his own feelings of grief, embarrassment, and anger, not to mention the fear of financial hardship. Meanwhile, his wife, Sarah, had her own fears and concerns. She, too, was worried about their financial future and felt compelled to pressure Ned to find a new job fast. As you might guess, this didn't always sit well with Ned, and soon Sarah became a target of his rage. Wanting to protect her family and their marriage,

Sarah was smart enough to give Ned time to calm down. Then, she once again insisted that he seek professional help.

Two weeks after being notified of his job loss, Ned finally contacted an outplacement firm and made an appointment with a counselor. Not only would Ned receive an updated resume and help with his networking and interviewing skills, he would also have a chance to review his entire career history, identify the skills that he most enjoyed using, and have the ongoing support he needed to turn this experience into a new, positive beginning.

The loss of his job shook Ned to his core. When I asked him if he could remember a point of reckoning he said, "Up until the time that I began working with the counselor, I was never very introspective. I worked, paid the bills, kept the house in good shape, and socialized with friends. Losing my job forced me to take a hard look at the way I was living my life. Not only did I have to look at where I was headed with my career, but I suddenly felt like I needed to examine other areas as well—my marriage, where I lived, my friendships, and my connection to my family. Prior to this experience, I rarely cried, got angry, or expressed any emotion at all. But, with the help of David, my counselor, I now feel like a totally different person. If someone had told me that losing my job would be a catalyst for so much positive change, I would have said they were crazy. But it's true. Believe it or not, losing my job was one of the best things that ever happened to me."

For Ned, losing his job was an unmistakable touch of grace. The jolt he received that day helped him see that he'd been sleepwalking through his life. This is what can happen when you step up to the plate and face difficult experiences head on and with open eyes. It opens the door to grace, and if you're ready, it will reveal to you a whole new way of being. An awakening of this kind usually also involves a period of emotional turmoil and sometimes, even physical pain. After all, once you step over the threshold, you're thrust into a kind of rebirth—a tumultuous process designed to return you to wholeness.

Think about your own life. Have you ever faced a challenge that turned out to be a blessing in disguise? What did this experience teach you?

———◆———

For me, the more self-aware I became, the more the tension between my fiancé and me increased. It was clear that something needed to change, but I couldn't stand the thought of being alone. Like so many women, I was more willing to tolerate inappropriate behavior and a mediocre relationship than to face the terror of being on my own. How would I support myself? What would I do with my time? What if I never met anyone again? It was obvious that I had made my relationship the focus of my life. I couldn't imagine my life without a man.

As I contemplated leaving my fiancé, I was hit with another blow—I lost my job. I had been working as an office manager for a real estate development company, and while I initially enjoyed my work, I had grown restless and bored. My heart wasn't in it anymore and I started to suffer from the Sunday night blues. I knew I needed to leave, but my position paid well and the work was easy. So, I stayed (another example of not listening to my inner voice). And then, shortly before my two-year anniversary with the company, I was informed that I was no longer needed. The company was downsizing and they let me go.

As cliché as it sounds, when it rains it pours was becoming a familiar phrase as I watched just about every area of my life get turned completely upside down. Not only was I facing the end of my relationship, I needed a new place to live, and a new job. All of this made me feel even more vulnerable, and I quickly started to backpedal about leaving my fiancé. I told myself that my standards were too high and I just needed to accept his humanness. In other words, if I could lower my expectations, things were sure to get better. So I took a job waiting tables, and put any thoughts of changing my life on hold.

It didn't work. My efforts to step back into my old life were a complete waste of time. That's because *a true call to consciousness*—a grace-inspired revelation—*is impossible to ignore or keep double-parked in the back of your mind.* Sure, you might stay in the same place for a while doing the same old things, but eventually the unsettled feeling of knowing that you're living a lie haunts your every move. That's what happened to me. I knew I was compromising my integrity, and I felt like a fraud. I could no longer sit in a bar drinking with my friends, pretend that I was in love, or deny the fact that I wanted to live a more healthy and balanced life. It was time to take responsibility for my life and get about the business of turning it around.

FINDING MY PRIORITIES

My first order of business was to find new work. While working in real estate development I learned a lot about the industry, and as a result, decided to get my real estate license so I could give sales a try. After getting my license, I took a job at a small office near my home. It was there that I met Kelly, a woman who would wind up being a god-send—just the right person at the right time to usher me through the door to a new life.

Kelly and I hit it off right away and got to know each other very quickly. Several nights a week we'd go to the local high school football field to walk around the track until we were physically, and sometimes even emotionally, drained. We took turns telling each other about our lives, dreams, and hopes for the future. Kelly talked about her childhood, the fact that she had grown up in an alcoholic home, and the effect that this had on her life. Years later, faced with a moment of truth herself, she found Al-Anon, and it initiated her own awakening to grace.

As Kelly shared the details of her life, I grew to trust her, and it inspired me to do the same. I talked about losing my job and the frustration of not knowing what I wanted to do with my life. I told her about my fiancé's drinking and my fear that our relationship was about to end. Kelly was the perfect person for me to confide in at this time in my life. As a woman who had her own share of challenges, she listened carefully to my story without judgment or criticism. Kelly gave me the kind of unconditional support we all need when faced with big changes. When we're in the wobbly stage of trying to stand on our own we need someone who is nonjudgmental and solid to lean on. By her example, Kelly taught me a powerful lesson about what it truly means to be a loving and compassionate friend. She never questioned my choices and she had a wonderful way of making me feel accepted. For the first time in years, I felt heard, valued, and respected.

Late one afternoon while walking around the track, I decided to talk more openly about the problems in my relationship and how they were affecting my life. "I live in a constant state of anxiety," I admitted. "I'm concerned about my fiancé's drinking. I don't know how much longer I can handle all the stress at home. I'm so tired of walking on eggshells trying to keep the peace."

When I finished, Kelly was silent for quite some time. Then, she gently suggested that I consider attending an Al-Anon meeting with her to see if it might provide some insight into my problem. She explained that the meetings were designed to support people whose lives were affected by alcohol and that I might find some valuable guidance and advice.

As difficult as my situation was, the idea of exposing the truth about my life to a group of strangers was unthinkable. Besides, to me, Alcoholics Anonymous and Al-Anon seemed to be for people whose lives were so deeply affected by alcohol that they were destitute or unable to keep a job. So, I politely declined, convinced that if I just tried harder and toughened up, I could keep my life on a steady course. Grace was tapping on my door, but I wasn't ready to answer.

When we're dealing with a situation that feels emotionally or physically threatening, it's normal to want to protect ourselves. We hunker down, don our emotional armor, and convince ourselves that we have everything under control.

But this is what gets us into trouble. Rather than use our experience as a springboard to being open to new ideas, or accepting offers of support, we choose behaviors that keep us from evolving. We do things like:

- Shut people out.
- Ignore advice or a different point of view.
- Refuse to ask for or receive help.
- Reject information that doesn't reflect our beliefs.
- Come up with excuses for why something won't work.
- Keep taking actions that haven't worked in the hopes that something will change.

Unfortunately, these behaviors make the experience of grace harder to see, or appreciate. For example, the Divine often speaks to us through the people in our lives, and when we ignore their wisdom or refuse an offer of support, we rob ourselves of the knowledge that could help us change our fate. In effect, we reject acts of grace.

A NEW BEGINNING

A few months passed and things got worse. As I started showing houses, I couldn't make a sale no matter how hard I worked. Things at home were becoming more chaotic as well. While I was doing my best to keep sane in an insane situation, I could no longer ignore the part of me that had awakened that night in the club. It was becoming more and more difficult to straddle both worlds. I felt like I was being chased by the truth and I was losing ground.

Looking back, I can see that my headstrong, driven personality prevented me from hitting my own bottom and reaching out for the help I needed. My pride and deep-seated insecurity had me tightly wrapped in a false sense of self. I desperately needed to believe that I had everything under control, otherwise my world would have fallen apart completely (not that it hadn't already come close). Eventually I would learn an important lesson—*surrender is the key that unlocks the door to grace*. Unfortunately, I kept trying all the wrong keys.

One Friday afternoon, my fiancé and I had a fight and he left the house angry. As I followed him out to his car, I tried to get him to stay and talk about the problem, but he refused. Instead, he left in a huff telling me not to wait up. As he pulled out of the driveway, I felt like an abandoned little girl. His abrupt departure pushed all my buttons and I was left feeling completely out of control.

The next morning when he still hadn't come home I called everyone I knew trying to find him. No one knew where he was. By day three I was down on my knees begging God to put an end to this madness. A few moments later, the phone rang and it was Kelly checking to see if he had come home yet. My response was immediate: "No. Let's go to a meeting." This decision would change the course of my life.

◆

My first Al-Anon meeting was held in the basement of a church. It was a Monday night in the fall of 1986, and I can still remember being terrified to get out of the car. What if I saw someone I knew? What was I supposed to say or do? I had no idea what to expect or what would be expected of me. When I finally got up enough courage to enter the meeting, I was surprised to find fifteen professionally dressed men and women sitting in a circle talking quietly to each other. Relieved that I didn't recognize anyone, I found a chair and sat down. As the meeting began, I promised myself I wouldn't say a word. Instead, I would simply listen.

For the next hour and a half, I sat mesmerized as each person shared a piece of *my* life story. One woman talked about her struggles with finding a career that she loved. Another was considering divorce and talked about her fear of being alone for the first time in her life. A lawyer, exhausted from trying to hold down a full-time job while managing the family at home, complained that he was fed up with his wife's drinking.

I couldn't believe what I was hearing. It was as if every single person in that room held a piece of my story and had shown up that evening to welcome me to the next phase of my life. A weight lifted from my shoulders as I began to see that I wasn't the only one whose life was falling apart. And I could see the healing in that room. It was obvious that the support and wisdom provided by the group had already helped many people achieve a far better life. The most encouraging message of all came during a conversation with a man who had been attending Al-Anon meetings for more than thirteen years. He said, "Once I admitted that my life was out of control and I was unable to fix it, doors seemed to open and the power of grace began to work its magic. Now, I wouldn't change a thing about my past. It led me to where I am today." I left the meeting that night filled with hope. I wanted a piece of that magic.

So, my awakening began in a nightclub and continued

in a church basement with a twelve-step group. As I started to admit that I needed help I felt like I had been thrown a life preserver. The love and support I received from the members of that group gave me the strength I needed to listen to and act on the wisdom of my inner voice.

Al-Anon happened to be the community that was right for me at this time in my life. As you begin your awakening process, you'll want to find a group that best supports *your* needs and inspires your personal growth. For example, you might join a men's group, a church group, a mother's group, or a therapist-led group; or even join or start a Life Makeover Group. The point is to find a community of people who are committed to becoming healthier and more conscious, human beings.

The first step of Al-Anon provided my key to a more conscious awareness of grace. I needed to face the reality that I was powerless to control or fix my life. Admitting that I didn't have the strength, knowledge, or ability to change my life was my first act of surrender. And as my good friend Jerry always says, "Surrender draws grace."

MOVING ON

After much thought and careful planning, I decided to break off my engagement and end our relationship. This decision forced me to focus on my basic needs—buying food, finding shelter, and earning a living. So I rented a home with three women to have an affordable place to live. Then, I got a job. I knew I needed to earn a living as quickly as possible, so I put my ego aside and worked as a temp to help pay my bills. And, I allowed myself to get the emotional care I needed to deal with the real source of my problems. Thankfully, I found a loving and compassionate therapist to help me uncover the reasons why I had gotten myself into this mess in the first place.

Over the next several months, I started to feel enormous pressure to decide what I wanted to do with my life. But, I refused to give in to it. Instead, I made one of the most important decisions of my life—*I would make my personal healing my number one priority*. This meant spending my hard-earned money on therapy, putting career dreams on hold, and engaging in the inner work that I'm sure many family members and friends saw as an unnecessary form of mental wheel spinning. But, I wanted to get to the core of what was driving my choices and behavior. What drove me to enter into dead-end relationships? Why did I continue to engage in behaviors that I knew were hurting me emotionally, physically, and spiritually? Why was I so concerned about what others thought of me, and why did I put everyone else's needs before my own?

This period of my life was deeply painful and at times, frightening. When we experience a revelation and finally make a decision to heed the call, there is a period of unraveling—a gradual peeling away of the many masks that have kept us hidden and safe. As these masks are stripped away, every emotion that's been concealed—fear, anger, or loneliness—rises to the surface. And, like a bandage that's removed from a wound, the exposure often leaves us feeling vulnerable and defenseless.

Fortunately, I didn't need to face this process alone. I was getting support from the new, healthy friendships I was forming with the people at meetings. This was a good thing considering that, as I continued my healing process, several old friendships started to deteriorate. The friends who used to enjoy my company at the local bar were not very comfortable with my choice to stop drinking. For some of them, having me around was like being forced to look into a mirror that reflected their own unsettling truths. This often happens when we begin to raise our level of consciousness. While it would be nice to take loved ones with us on the journey, the reality is that we all grow and evolve at our own pace. It's one of the main reasons why so many people stay stuck in unsatisfying lives—they're afraid of how their relationships will change. Well, here's the truth: you *will* lose people as you grow and heal. It's a natural part of the process. But, the good news is that the healthier you become, the more you start to attract friends and colleagues who are aligned with your level of consciousness.

Having found a like-minded community, my involvement in Al-Anon became a safe haven for me to express my growing self-awareness, and I developed several new friendships with people who shared my desire for a better quality of life. This made saying goodbye to old friends a little less painful. The support from these new relationships also helped me look more closely at what needed to change. It became apparent to me that my greatest fear was of being alone. When I look back, I can see that this affected almost every decision I made at this time in my life. It would take one more frustrating, long-term relationship to finally muster the courage to face this fear head-on. On some level I knew that until I lived alone, without any romantic relationship to distract me from the inner healing that needed to be done, I would keep repeating old patterns that would hinder my personal growth.

YOUR MOMENT OF TRUTH

There is an amazing gift waiting for you on the other side of your moment of truth. It's the gift of grace. The areas of your life that are begging for attention are offering you an invitation. And, because you've picked up this book, there's a good chance you may be ready to accept. When you do, you set in motion a gradual awakening to a benevolent source of energy that will guide your next steps. Once you learn to trust this process, you'll have the courage to take action sooner rather than later. To many of us, it feels frightening to question our marriage, face the reality that we're in debt, or leave a job that's robbing us of passion and energy. But it doesn't have to. Often, at our most trying hour, an experience of grace lets us know that all will be well and that we're *not* alone.

Consider Evan's story. At the time of his awakening, or wake-up call, as he said, Evan was twenty-one years old. He was finishing his undergrad degree in business and was considering getting his MBA. Evan's dad was the president of a small retail clothing chain and had asked him to join the company once he finished school. Unsure of what he wanted for the future, and not wanting to disappoint his dad, Evan agreed. Now he was questioning his decision.

One afternoon while at a friend's home, Evan had an unsettling experience. He was sitting in the living room by himself while his friend was on the phone in another room. Outside, there were several men painting the house, and as

Evan watched them work he suddenly had the feeling that he was being painted *into* the house. Recalling the event, he said, "I remember thinking, it was such an odd feeling. I started to feel anxious and claustrophobic." As this feeling persisted, Evan got up and tried to shake it off, but the feeling only intensified. He then went outside for some fresh air and was surprised to discover that his feeling of being trapped got worse. "I felt like the world was closing in on me," he described, "and the only thing I knew in that moment was that I needed to find a safe place."

Without telling his friend, Evan immediately got in his car and headed home. Minutes later, he saw his older brother, Chuck, driving toward him. Chuck was the one person Evan trusted and could talk to about anything. He was surprised to see him, and quickly waved him over to the side of the road. Shaken and embarrassed, Evan started to tell Chuck what was happening. His brother listened intently and then asked Evan to sit in his car. Once they were settled, Chuck revealed that he and his dad had noticed that Evan seemed a bit distant lately, even depressed. As a matter of fact, they had just been discussing this the night before, and thought it would be a good idea for Chuck to check in with Evan to see what was going on.

As Evan listened to Chuck, his eyes welled up with tears. All of his fears and conflicting feelings about what he was doing (or not doing) with his life poured out. He expressed his concern about the future, whether or not he should go on to graduate school, and his fear of disappointing his dad. Chuck assured Evan that his father only wanted what was best for him and suggested that they get together that evening to talk more about what was going on.

The fact that Evan's brother Chuck, the only family member he felt safe with, showed up when he did is an example of how grace often intervenes when we need it most. As you listen to what Evan has to say years later, take special note of his language. It's a beautiful example of how our souls attempt to get our attention through the use of images or metaphors that reflect a truth we need to face. "When I look back fifteen years ago to the episode at my friend's house, it's amazing to think something that felt in no way graceful, now feels like a tremendous gift. I see my confusion and depression as the nudge I needed to live a bigger, more rewarding life. If I hadn't had that awakening, my life would have been much smaller and more contained. All along I was doing what was expected of me, and in order to heal, I needed to step out of the picture I had painted myself into. I had no idea what *my* life looked like, but I was ready to find out. Thank God Chuck showed up at the time and place I needed him most."

Is there a place in your life where you feel painted into a corner? Who can you turn to for advice or support?

Sometimes a moment of truth isn't so dramatic. For no apparent reason, we make a decision while going about the normal business of our daily lives. One moment you're on your way to work and the next you hear yourself say, "Enough is enough." For Alyssa, a hardworking mother of two, that's exactly what happened. Here's what she had to say:

"Every morning I commuted to New York City by ferry. I'd wake up in the dark, get dressed, and drive to the parking lot at the harbor. I followed the same routine for years, working long hours almost every day. Then one spring morning, everything changed. As I sat on the ferry watching the sunrise, I was deeply moved. For some reason, at that moment—the crisp morning air, the color in the distant sky, and the hypnotic hum of the boat, made me stop and ask, 'Is this all I'm meant to do? Get up every morning and travel by ferry to work, day in and day out?' The moment I pondered this question, the answer became crystal clear: 'You're meant to do something more meaningful and satisfying with your life.'

"From that moment on I started to notice things that I had never noticed before. I started to see the birds outside my window. I began to pay more attention to my dog, to my friends, and to my family. I had fallen into a rut and as a result, was living an empty, colorless life. It wasn't until that morning on the ferry, that I realized what I was missing. It was like I woke up and decided that I deserved, even craved, something more."

Alyssa's experience is an example of how a grace-filled moment can heighten our sensitivity. As we become more conscious, we not only see what's not working in our lives, but also become more aware of what is. And it's the recognition of beauty, companionship, or a connection to the natural world, that motivates us to move forward with change in spite of our self-doubt and fear.

———◆———

While speaking to people about the events that led to their moments of truth, more often than not, I've found that these events were fueled by the pain of living a lie. For some, the truth was masked by an addiction, for example, to alcohol, gambling, drugs, shopping, or food. For others, it's a health crisis—depression, chronic pain, or the onset of a serious illness. In all cases, though, there's a common theme; most people, in one way or another, are living someone else's life rather than their own. Striving to meet the expectations of others, we suppress vital energy that ends up expressing itself in a distorted or self-destructive way.

Throughout our lives we are continually presented with opportunities to take ownership of our own lives. When we recognize these opportunities for what they really are, we see that they offer us a choice—to go back to sleep or to wake up and move to another level of consciousness. If we choose the latter, we become more open to, and cognizant of, the presence of grace in our everyday lives.

My awakening in the nightclub many years ago was my first recognition of grace. It opened the door to an amazing path of self-discovery that changed my life forever. As you continue on this journey, you'll discover that you can change yours, too!

Experiment: Opening Your Life to Grace

This experiment is designed to help you open the door to grace. Take out your journal and answer the following questions:

- Is there a problem area of your life that needs to change? If so, which area is it?
- How might you be blocking grace? What are you doing to control the situation?
- If you were ready to surrender, what would you need to do (or stop doing) to let go of control?
- Next, imagine a graceful ending or outcome to this problem and describe what happens.

• Who can support you while you begin making this change? Is there someone in your life who is nonjudgmental, patient, and sensitive to your needs?

Once you've answered the questions, write the following prayer in your journal and repeat it out loud:

> *I am now open and receptive to the power of grace in my life. I ask to be shown clear examples of how I can face this challenge with courage, wisdom, and strength.*

Repeat this prayer throughout the day. See it drawing toward you the exact support, resources, and guidance you need to get on the path of change. Pay close attention to any signs or messages you receive and be sure to write about them in your journal.

Resources

BOOKS

From Panic to Power by Lucinda Bassett (Harper Resource, 1997)

> *If you're dealing with anxiety, fear, depression, or panic, Lucinda's guidance will be a big help. I recommend her work often.*

Spiritual Divorce: Divorce as a Catalyst for an Extraordinary Life by Debbie Ford (Harper San Francisco, 2001)

> *If you're going through (or contemplating) divorce, this is an important book on how to use divorce as a catalyst for positive change. It's a great resource for dealing with the emotional ups and downs (anger at your ex, fear of being alone, and so on) of this transition.*

To Hell and Back: Healing Your Way Through Transition by Gail Kauranen Jones (Hats Off Books, 2004)

> *A book that guides baby boomers through a variety of life-altering events.*

Transitions: Making Sense of Life's Changes by William Bridges (Perseus Books Group, 1980)

> *A resource that's been around for some time, this book offers helpful strategies for dealing with difficult, painful, and confusing times in your life.*

WEBSITES

www.aa.org

> *This is the Alcoholics Anonymous World Services website. Alcoholics Anonymous is an organization dedicated to helping men and women achieve sobriety.*

www.al-anon.alateen.org

> *Dedicated to offering hope and help to families and friends of alcoholics.*

www.GriefNet.org

> *This is an Internet community of people dealing with grief, death, and major loss. Lots of great resources here.*

www.mentalhelp.net

> *This site provides a comprehensive source of online mental health information, news, and resources.*

www.stresscenter.com

> *Lucinda Bassett's website about attacking anxiety and depression.*

2

---◆---

EMBARK ON A SPIRITUAL JOURNEY

WHEN WE OPEN THE DOOR TO GRACE, life as we've known it will start to change. For some, this process is profound—relationships end, careers are overhauled, or a geographical move is in order. For others, the change is less monumental and may involve a single area of their lives. After my experience in the nightclub, I had two of the most painful, and meaningful years of my life. I felt like a child who had suddenly opened her eyes to a frightening new world—a world that felt harsh, unfamiliar, and lonely. As I tentatively left my former life behind, I began the long, slow process of waking up. Looking back I can see that choosing to wake up is one of the most courageous decisions we ever make. *Today I thank God that my pain was greater than my fear.*

The process of awakening that follows a moment of truth is a gradual unfolding of a more conscious way of life. During this period we begin to ask some fundamental questions: Who am I? Why am I here? Who's benefiting most from the choices I make? Am I living *my* life or fol-

49

lowing someone else's agenda? We also begin to assess how we feel about critical areas of our lives and consider the changes that may be warranted.

The road can be a rocky one. We stumble and fall, get back up, and continue to forge ahead searching for answers in a variety of places—books, workshops, our religion, or conversations with others. All of these avenues lead us deeper into our selves, our history, and our healing, and ultimately the hard work pays off. Our emotional health improves and we set the stage for a spiritual awakening that allows grace to influence our lives in an even greater way.

GETTING ON THE ROAD

After leaving my fiancé, I moved into a beautiful Victorian home with my sister Michelle and two friends. I became increasingly more involved in Al-Anon and continued to see a therapist, sifting through my past in an effort to know and understand myself better. Most days I felt like I was living in a whirlwind, moving in and out of the eye of the storm. One moment I felt happy and at peace about my new life, and the next I felt lonely and terrified.

During this period, I reestablished an important habit I developed as a young girl. At the age of twelve I started keeping what was then called a diary. I wrote pages of poetry, copied favorite quotes and passages from books, and eventually, as I overcame my fear that someone might find and read what I was writing, I started to record my feelings and thoughts as well. Over time though, I became so preoccupied with school, boys, friends, and my social life that I lost interest in keeping a diary. By the time I picked this habit back up many years later, my diary was called a journal, and it would become the single most important tool I would use to awaken my life to the influence of grace.

As soon as I started writing, I felt as though I was reconnecting with an old friend. I poured myself into my journal. I wrote about how lonely I felt, and my fear of dying before I did all I wanted to do. I fantasized about letting go of the self-consciousness that kept the real me trapped inside. At first, my entries were more intellectual than emotional. In fact, many times I was conscious of writing *around* the truth. I was so used to being who others wanted me to be that I couldn't even be honest with myself. As I read these pages twenty-five years later, I have such compassion for the young woman who was struggling to find her place in the world.

Keeping a journal or notebook can provide some critical and surprising insights—how you approach and respond to difficult situations, patterns of thinking that serve you or get you into trouble, or reoccurring feelings that reflect a problem you've been blind to, or in denial about. Sometimes it's easier to be honest on paper as opposed to trying to verbalize your thoughts. Keeping a journal also sends an important message to your soul, one that says, "I value myself, and the choice I've made to live a more authentic life so I will give you my time and attention."

If I told you that writing in a journal three or four times a week, for just twenty minutes at a time, would improve your ability to recognize and respond to the influence of grace, wouldn't it be worth a try? Believe me, it will give you a more objective perspective of what's working and not working in your life. Keeping a journal will enable you to connect and stay connected to your true feelings and desires. You'll open a channel for Divine wisdom to help you see and decode the messages that are meant to be guideposts for your life. Finally, and most importantly, as we take note of and record these guideposts, we strengthen our faith that there is a higher plan for our lives.

When you think about keeping a journal, don't feel pressured to write in it everyday. There is no rule of thumb about how often you need to write to be a good journal keeper. Just write. Also, if you have any concern whatsoever about someone reading it, be sure to keep your journal in a safe place (under lock and key if necessary). Otherwise, you'll start editing your entries and avoid the truth—the kiss of death for journal writing.

FINDING YOUR OWN WAY

The journal that works for you may not involve writing at all. My friend Kate rekindled her love of art to assist in her self-discovery process. At the age of forty-five she had experienced a moment of truth when she was diagnosed with a serious form of skin cancer. While her prognosis was good, Kate said that the shock of being faced with her mortality motivated her to honor her inner artist. Three months after her diagnosis, Kate made a decision to move to a small town outside of Santa Fe, New Mexico, to pursue her love of watercolor art. The beauty and openness of the Southwest gave her inspiration and a feeling of expansiveness that had been missing from her life for years. She picked up a full-time job in a bookstore and started painting at night and on weekends. Kate said that downshifting her lifestyle allowed her to totally immerse herself in her art and provided her with a whole new form of self-expression.

"I painted what was alive within me. At the end of each day I'd go into my small studio, light a candle, and begin by splashing color on a canvas. I kept each painting, and when I was done, dated the artwork and added it to what I called my personal portfolio. I had a large open space in my bedroom, and at the end of the week I would place each painting side by side on the floor and view them as one whole body of work. This allowed me to see the bigger picture. I could see my dark days in paintings with grays, blacks, and deep blues, whereas good days were reflected by those with brighter, more vibrant colors. The process of painting my inner landscape allowed my art to come alive and served as a sort of visual journal. I like to think of each canvas as a stepping-stone on a journey that returned me to my real self."

How might you get to know yourself in a more intimate way? Think about it. What form might you use for your own journal? Will you take photographs? Write poems? Set up a weekly conversation with a friend to share your thoughts and feelings?

FINDING THE SOURCE OF HEALING

Healing doesn't happen in our heads. It happens in our hearts as we learn to connect with our feelings. This usually means dealing with uncomfortable emotions first—the ones we've stuffed inside or ignored. When it was time for me to face my own emotions, I proceeded with caution and care. Like so many of us who fall asleep and live life in a comfortably numb place, I was completely disconnected from how I felt. I can still remember one afternoon during a counseling session, when my therapist issued a challenge. "Cheryl, every time I ask you to tell me how you feel, you start *reporting* about your life. You're so good at intellectualizing everything. I want you to stop for a moment, close your eyes, and tell me how you *feel*."

As I tried to connect with something, *anything,* the only thing I felt was awkward and uncomfortable. The truth was, I couldn't put words to any feelings at all. My ability to *feel* had been conveniently turned off by my unconscious lifestyle, my drinking, and the habits and behaviors I learned as a child. If I felt anything at all, it was usually because I was experiencing some kind of strong emotion like panic, deep sadness, or frustration. To avoid the discomfort and messiness of emotions, I had learned to live from the neck up.

We are an emotionally phobic culture. The world we live in practically requires us to disengage from our feelings in order to survive. Voice mail; e-mail; violence; seductive or threatening news; these are the kinds of things that desensitize us by causing neural overload. Moreover, it's often easier to stay asleep than to deal with the reality of how unsatisfying our lives really are. If we *could* feel, many of us couldn't tolerate the lives we're living.

But to feel is to truly be alive. As Robert A. Johnson, author of *The Fisher King and the Handless Maiden,* says: "Thinking is that cool faculty which brings clarity and objectivity—but provides no valuing; sensation describes the physical world—but provides no valuing; intuition suggests a wide range of possibilities—but provides no valuing. Only feeling brings a sense of value and worth; indeed, this is its chief function. Without feeling there is no value judgment. To lose one's feeling function is thus to lose one of the most precious human faculties, perhaps the one that makes us most human."

Learning to connect my head with my heart required a great deal of patience and perseverance. Thankfully Al-Anon gave me a safe place to start. The assurance of anonymity, along with the fact that members are required to listen to one another rather than offer opinions or advice, made it easier to be vulnerable and honest about what was happening in my life. As I reflect on this time, I can see that these meetings provided each of us with an opportunity to do something most people rarely have a chance to do—tell our life stories. Men and women of all ages, professions, ethnicities, and religious affiliations would come to these meetings week after week. They would empty the intimate details of their lives into the middle of this sacred space only to be received with warmth, understanding, and compassion. I discovered, as so many have before and since, that the telling of one's story in a safe environment is in fact one of the most powerful ways to heal.

When I first started to attend meetings, I would sit in the back of the room to avoid being seen. The group's emphasis on being open and honest made me feel extremely vulnerable, and I knew that my eyes would reveal the emotions I wasn't quite ready to share. As I listened to others tell their stories, there were countless times when I felt touched by an experience of grace, as though God was speaking directly to me through the brave men and women who were challenging the legacy of pain passed onto them by the previous generation.

Over time, the courage I witnessed in these meetings started to rub off, encouraging me to share my own story. The rigid walls I had built around my heart began to soften as I learned to let people in. I was lucky. A core group of us showed up every week to share in each other's healing journey. It provided us with a kind of healthy family that made it easier to make the difficult changes we all knew we needed to make. The support I received from these men and women allowed me to begin straightening out my crooked life. I began to believe I had choices. I began to believe I could change.

Today, after spending many years traveling around the country speaking to thousands of people about their lives, I've learned that our deepest need as human beings is to be seen and heard. We want to know that we matter. Rarely do we have a chance to sit in a room with compassionate and understanding witnesses who allow us to share our most private thoughts and feelings. Al-Anon gave me this gift. Telling my story, piece by small piece, filled this basic human need for me in a way that was profoundly healing.

While working on this book, I once again witnessed the powerful healing effect of sharing one's personal story. I invited a small group of people to my home to discuss their experiences with grace. The group included men and women, single and married, who ranged in age from thirty to seventy-five years old. My guests also represented a wide variety of spiritual beliefs and backgrounds, including a born-again Christian, an atheist, a Buddhist, and those who considered their spiritual beliefs and practices to be more eclectic in nature. For more than five hours we talked about a variety of topics—how we each defined grace, our religious histories, and examples of how grace had touched our lives.

While the conversation was rich with wisdom and insight, what struck me most was the level of emotion that welled up in each person as they got deeper and deeper into the details of their lives. It was clear that the more their experiences were received with unconditional love and respect, the safer they felt to let their guard down. And from this place of vulnerability and authenticity, we all experienced a deeply intimate connection—a form of grace in and of itself. Later that night, as I lay in bed thinking about the gathering, I felt a longing for more of this kind of spiritual dialogue in my own life.

While journaling and Al-Anon were the first tools I used to support my quest for truth and self-understanding, my friend Margaret went about it in a totally different way. When Margaret found herself on the other side of a moment of truth, she felt lost and unsure of what to do next. But, she knew what she didn't want. She had no desire to go back to the 24-7 lifestyle she led as a professional musician on the road.

One night at dinner, a friend recommended a book she thought Margaret would like. She had just finished reading *Living in the Light* by Shakti Gawain and raved about how much it helped her to see her life from a more spiritual and empowered perspective. She strongly recommended that Margaret read the book.

Several weeks later, Margaret had forgotten all about her friend's recommendation. But, much to her surprise, the book appeared in her mailbox with a note from her friend that read, "Something told me to send this to you. In case you hadn't picked it up yet, I thought I'd send one your way." Although Margaret didn't realize it at the time, grace was gently guiding her to her next step.

Margaret sat down in her living room and opened the book to read the first page. Twenty-four hours later, she finished it. By this time, several pages were dog-eared, and numerous passages were either highlighted or underlined. Margaret was so inspired by the book's message that, for the next year, it became what she called her manual for life. "It was the right book at the right time," she said. "It answered so many of the questions that were rolling around in my head. For me, almost every word had special meaning. That book became a roadmap for the next phase of my life."

For many people, books are a conduit for grace. They open our hearts and minds to new ways of thinking and being in the world. My client Marsha had a little ritual that she found helpful during her own awakening process. Every Saturday, she would visit the religion section of her local bookstore, say a prayer asking to be guided to the right book, and then choose one off the shelf. Then she would sit in the café and read. Marsha called this ritual her date with God, and the insights she received helped her trust that a Higher Power was guiding her to the resources that best served her personal and spiritual growth. She always ended up reading something that addressed her current situation.

I too have read books that appeared at a time when I needed them most. For example, a book by Anne Wilson Schaef called *Codependence: Misunderstood—Mistreated,* provided me with several *aha* experiences that allowed me to understand why I behaved the way I did in my relationships with men. Books by John Bradshaw such as *Healing the Shame that Binds You* and *Bradshaw on the Family,* did the same thing. They gave me valuable insights that were useful as I explored the world of addiction and the recovery process. I was especially drawn to motivational classics such as *The Power of Positive Thinking* by Norman Vincent Peale, *The Game of Life and How to Play It* by Florence Scovel Shinn, *Think and Grow Rich* by Napoleon Hill, and *As a Man Thinketh* by James Allen. These books combined spiritual concepts with practical advice, and I appreciated the fact that they offered readers specific, tangible ways to implement their strategies. Looking back, I can see that the resources, events, and people who appear during our soul journey often hold clues to our future endeavors. These spiritual classics most influenced my writing and teaching later on.

I'm sure you've had similar experiences. You come across a book at your local bookstore that seems interesting, or you get a recommendation from a friend. Then, once you get into it, you find yourself scrambling for a pen to underline passages. Over the years there have been many times that clients have come to our coaching sessions excited about a book that helped them gain a new perspective. It's a good example of how some people experience grace—they are given the right message at the right time.

Many people who begin a soul journey also use workshops and seminars to raise their levels of consciousness and self-awareness. Often when I finished a book that had a great impact on me, I made a point to look for a workshop led by the author. Because my resources were limited, I wanted to be sure that I was spending my time and money on programs that would serve my needs best. Reading a book beforehand gave me the assurance I needed. Fortunately, Internet access now makes the process of finding high-quality workshops much easier.

During this period, there was one workshop in particular that added a unique dimension to my work. After attending a program by Marion Woodman, a Jungian analyst who, at the time, had written *Addiction to Perfection* and *Pregnant Virgin,* I started recording my dreams in my journal. Marion delivered a program on the healing power of dreams, and watching her teach was inspiring. Her lecture was magical, filled with images and metaphors that made her material come to life. That day, I discovered another powerful way for the Divine to support our efforts to live a more conscious life—by communicating with us through our dreams. I left the workshop with a firm commitment to begin a dream journal—a notebook that would capture my nightly travels.

There was just one problem—I never remembered my dreams. As a matter of fact, several of us in the workshop were convinced that we didn't dream at all. Marion assured us that everyone had the potential to dream, and that once we began to write down whatever we could remember upon wakening, our subconsciouses would get the message that we were paying attention. As a result, our dreams would become vivid and accessible. Sure enough, within a few short weeks of writing down dream fragments, I began to have the most amazing insights. For example, several months after breaking off my engagement, I was having a hard time getting emotionally unhooked from the relationship. I was angry about how I allowed myself to be treated and often replayed painful scenes in my mind. I kept wishing I had done something different. One night, I had a powerful dream that put an end to this self-defeating behavior. Here is the entry from my journal:

> *I'm back in the home I shared with my fiancé. I'm washing dirty laundry in the basement. As I put the wet clothes into the dryer, I'm thinking about all the times I allowed myself to be treated with disrespect. I'm angry and disappointed with myself. Suddenly, I feel a presence. When I look up, I see what feels like a higher self who says, "You're being much too hard on yourself, Cheryl. Get out of the basement. It's okay to move on."*

I woke up feeling empowered. Because the dream was so direct and timely, I felt like I had been blessed with a gift of clarity and courage. From that day forward, I stopped beating myself up, and the practice of working with my dreams (something I still do to this day) became another method of opening my mind to Divine wisdom.

What might your dreams be trying to tell you? To find out, keep your journal or notebook by your bed and start jotting down even the slightest recollections. Record any thoughts, feelings, words, or images that come to mind. If you can remember enough of a dream, write it out and give it a title. Ask yourself, "What's the primary theme or message of this dream?" Then, write the first thing that comes to mind at the top of the page. Don't overanalyze your answer. Trust your subconscious to give you the information you need. Once you have a title, remember it and think about it throughout the day. Holding the title in mind keeps the dream alive and is a great way to gain additional insight. Over time, as you continue to keep track of your dreams, there's a good chance that you'll start to see patterns or messages that will prove increasingly helpful.

Often during our awakening to grace, we find ourselves doing things we never imagined doing. For example, my client James, an engineer from the Midwest, did something that to him was unthinkable. Having gone through a painful divorce that left him single after twenty years of marriage, he signed up for a men's retreat. Sharing his innermost thoughts and feelings was considered taboo in James's family. And if you absolutely had to discuss something, you certainly didn't do it with strangers, let alone pay money to do so. But James was devastated. His wife had left him for another man, and after two years, he still couldn't get on with his life.

During the retreat, James was surrounded by men who empathized with his situation. On the second day, he was given a chance to talk about his divorce in front of the group. James was angry. He had worked hard to support his family and was proud of the fact that he had always provided them with a comfortable home and lifestyle. James couldn't understand what he'd done to warrant this act of betrayal.

As he talked about his confusion and frustration, he became even more enraged. Nobody moved or made a sound. The men continued to provide a safe container for James to express his feelings. After twenty or thirty minutes into his tirade, he started to sob. Now the group was listening to James talk about striving to get straight As in school, graduating from college at the top of his class, and working his butt off to land an executive position at the age of

twenty-eight. All in an effort to gain his father's approval—
something he rarely got, regardless of what he achieved.

James was beginning to see that he was repeating the
same patterns in his marriage. He considered himself a
great dad and a loyal husband. His work ethic made him a
solid contributor to his family, yet his job kept him so busy
that, when he was home, he rarely spent quality time with
his wife. James didn't know how to slow down or relax. If
he wasn't always in motion, doing something productive,
he felt lazy and worthless. Meanwhile, his wife found someone else to meet her long-ignored needs.

During the retreat, James discovered that at the root of
all his activity was a little boy who was still trying to get his
dad's approval. But his wife's affair suddenly changed his
perspective of what determined his worth. His attempt to
win her approval and love by maintaining his status as the
dependable, successful breadwinner hadn't worked. The
workshop helped James to see the bigger picture. To have a
healthy, viable, intimate relationship, he needed to understand that his time and attention was more valuable than
any material things he could provide for his family.

The love and support he received from the men at the
retreat was an enormous gift of grace. It was exactly what
he needed to begin the process of moving on and repairing
his life. Although James admitted to feeling vulnerable and
a little foolish afterward, he said the relief he experienced
was well worth the discomfort. At the end of the retreat, he
made a decision to go into therapy—something he never
would have considered before having this experience.

Therapy can play a critical role in helping us open our
lives to grace for three important reasons: First, the process

of uncovering the underlying reasons for our dysfunctional behavior allows us to dismantle the defense mechanisms we put in place to protect us from our pain. These blocks—denial and control for example—prevent us from tapping into the power of grace. Second, good therapy pulls us into the present and helps us to face the truth so we can stop seeing our lives as we want them to be, and instead, see them as they really are. Having someone witness our life gives us a more honest perspective that helps break the chain of denial. Third, therapy also provides a safety net as we begin to relinquish control.

At the point that I began my work in therapy, too much of my time and energy was spent trying to manage the perceptions of the people around me. When we're afraid, we often attempt to manipulate our environment—people, situations, and events—to feel safe and in charge. This meant that I rarely told the truth about how I felt or what I needed in a given situation. Instead, I'd turn myself into a human pretzel trying to be who I thought others wanted me to be. I remember when a counselor asked, "Cheryl, what do *you* need?" and I couldn't give her an answer. I sat back in the chair, staring off into space like some kind of frozen mummy. I was stumped. I had spent so much time focused on what others needed that I had no idea what I wanted for myself.

I left the office that day with homework—identify my needs and come back to my next session with a list. As simple as this may sound, the assignment wasn't easy. I had let someone in closer than ever before and I was feeling some resistance. The honesty and intimacy that therapy demands challenges us to confront our vulnerability—not an easy thing for most of us to do. When someone peels back the covers of our bravado or false pride, and we're challenged to admit the truth, it's not uncommon to suddenly search for reasons to back out of the relationship. There were several times when I almost quit therapy. But over time I learned that when we feel exposed we're simply being given an opportunity to take a giant step forward—closer to the truth, not further away.

That afternoon when I returned home from my therapist's office, I hung a large message board on the wall in my living room and put a marker nearby. Each time I walked by, I made a point to stop and ask myself what I needed in that moment. At first, my entries started with simple things like a nap, something to eat, or a cup of tea. Then as I continued this practice, my answers began to reflect deeper needs. I was lonely and needed the companionship of a good friend. I was afraid of not being able to pay my bills and needed a secure source of income. Sometimes I downplayed the importance of nonessential needs. For example, at one point I realized that my bedroom felt stark and uncomfortable. I needed to warm it up with decorations that made it feel homey and inviting.

Writing my needs on the message board in my living room was one example of how my work with a therapist was teaching me new life skills. By doing this exercise, I was starting to find a balance between loving and caring for others and loving and caring for myself.

Too often therapy is seen as unnecessary or self-indulgent. Yet from my experience both personally and in working with clients, it can be a vital means of supporting our psychological and spiritual development. First, it teaches us compassion, both for each other and ourselves. When we understand that many choices we make are the result of our conditioning and level of consciousness at the time, we develop empathy for ourselves, knowing that we did the best we could with the resources we had at the time. And from this place, we recognize that others are doing the best they can, too.

Good therapy also challenges us to grow up. As we face the reality that we're the ones in charge of our lives, we stop blaming others. We can no longer claim the role of victim as we learn to take full responsibility for our actions and their consequences. And as difficult as it may be to commit to seeing the truth and living with integrity, we also reap the rewards. Life becomes multidimensional, filled with rich relationships and meaningful experiences. Rather than being emotionally phobic—afraid of our feelings—good therapy teaches us to embrace them. By doing this, we release an enormous amount of pent-up energy that we use to keep feelings locked inside. And we strengthen our ability to love and connect with others.

What tools have you used during your own self-discovery process? Think about it. Have you read books, attended workshops, or kept a journal? What haven't you tried yet that might help you access hidden parts of yourself? Would seeing a therapist be a good idea for you at this time in your life? If so, make sure you find a good one. Ask for referrals from family members and friends, or the professionals who provide you with health care services (doctor, massage therapist, nurse practitioner). Once you find a therapist, be sure to interview him or her before making a decision. Ask the following questions:

- What is your education, background, and professional experience?
- How long have you been in practice?
- Have you been in therapy yourself?
- What types of clients and issues do you normally deal with?
- What methods or models do you use?

Describe your situation and ask for examples of how they might work with you. Don't settle for someone who seems okay. Be willing to interview as many people as you need to find your best possible fit.

SEEING THE LIGHT OF GRACE

As I continued to heal and to get my life in order, something strange began to happen. Little coincidences seemed to occur at the precise moment when I needed encouragement. For example, I'd show up at an Al-Anon meeting in a bad mood, feeling scared about my financial situation, only to discover that the topic of the meeting was choosing courage over fear. This gave me a chance to hear several people talk about how they had learned to replace fear with faith. Or I'd decide to leave a meeting halfway through because something someone said hit too close to home, and at the break, someone would ask me to help clean up when the meeting was over. There were countless times when I longed to slip back into my old unconscious life, only to be saved by the inspiring story of someone who stayed the course. Witnessing the stories of others restored my belief that my future held something far greater than my past.

The coincidences were happening outside of the meetings as well. As one temporary job would end, another would appear within a week to provide the income I needed to pay my bills. When a friend who no longer shared my values dropped out of my life, a new friend who supported and even encouraged my growth would appear. These mini-miracles weren't just happening to me, they were happening to other group members as well.

One woman I met at a meeting shared an example of how her husband received some unexpected support during a difficult time. After years of abusing alcohol, he had finally gone into a recovery program. A few weeks before entering rehab, he hired a new secretary. Her first day on the job was the day he was admitted for treatment. One of the first phone calls he made from rehab was to tell her where he was and that he would be out of the office for a month. During the call he discovered that she had been in AA for several years. Her understanding and support allowed him to be open about his recovery during a sensitive time of his life. And eventually it gave him the flexibility he needed to work AA meetings into his schedule without the pressure of trying to keep his activities confidential.

During my years as a coach, I've been a witness to hundreds of similar experiences. When clients wake up and take action to make positive changes in their lives, a Higher Power intercedes on their behalf. It's as though a new door slowly opens and the light of grace shines through to illuminate the path. My client Kevin described this process well:

"Before I began to straighten out my life, I would not have considered myself a spiritual person. But as I committed to healing my relationships, my past, and the areas of my current life that needed to change, things seemed to come together in unexpected ways. It was as if someone or something was behind the scenes helping to make things easier.

"I remember one day in particular when I decided to have a frank conversation with my father about his verbally abusive behavior. In the past, when we attempted to get together, there were often problems—travel delays, his bad mood, or circumstances that prevented me from meeting with him alone. On this day, things were different. Everything went smoothly. When I arrived at his office, he was in an unusually open and receptive mood. Then one of his clients canceled an appointment at the last minute giving us the whole afternoon together. I remember thinking to myself, Well, isn't this strange. It's as if all the obstacles are being taken out of my path so I can have this conversation."

In the beginning, it's tempting to see these coincidences as luck, chance, or fate. But over time it becomes clear that something more important is going on. They are inspired events designed to show us that a Higher Power is guiding us as we hold steadfast to our commitment to remain conscious and grow. *Our willingness to do the work to become more conscious is what paves the way for us to recognize the unmistakable touch of grace.*

———◆———

During the next several years, my life improved dramatically. At first, I focused on the basics—creating a home that felt safe and comfortable, paying off debt, learning to live well within my means. I also gave up alcohol and started exercising and eating healthier food. This allowed me to begin living *in* my body instead of rejecting it. As I built a strong foundation to support my new life, the coincidences continued. And, as you'll see, at times they were pretty dramatic. During the next phase of my adventure I began to pay even more attention. Like a private investigator searching for evidence, I set out to confirm the existence of a Higher Power in my own life. It didn't take long. I got the proof I needed.

Experiment: Tell Your Story

This experiment is designed to help you experience the healing power of telling your story by revisiting your spiritual history. While you can complete this experiment on your own by writing in your journal, doing it with a partner will have a far greater effect.

1. Choose someone you trust who is a great listener and who makes you feel safe. If you'd like to meet others who are looking for comrades, please visit our Life Makeover Community online (www.cherylrichardson.com). You'll find the resources you need to locate people in your hometown. I can assure you that there are people similar to you who want to connect with like-minded friends.

2. Explain this experiment and invite the person you trust to complete the assignment with you. Then, set a date to get together to share your stories once you've completed them.

3. Separate your life thus far into three parts and assign a "spiritual headline" that best represents the overall theme of each one. It could be something like, "My Early

Religious Years," "A Crisis in Faith," or "How I Made a New Relationship with God."

4. Once you finish the headlines, tell the story of each part using a format that suits you best. You might write your story, paint your story, use photographs, or even create a scrapbook that combines images with words. Use some of the following questions as a guide to make your story-telling easier:

   a. What was the state of your spiritual life during this period?
   b. What religious training, if any, did you receive?
   c. What relevant events occurred?
   d. Who were the people who most influenced your spiritual beliefs at the time?
   e. How did you care for your spirit? What rituals did you love?
   f. What were your parents' attitudes toward religion or spirituality and how did they affect you?
   g. What family or cultural messages did you receive about life that might influence your understanding or acceptance of grace? For example, if your parents were unsuccessful at fulfilling your needs, you may have internalized a message that says "It's not realistic to expect help," making it difficult to believe in the idea of Divine support.

If you have trouble remembering your early life, use photographs or items from a keepsake box to help jog your memory. Take as much time as you need to complete this part of the experiment.

5. Tell your story. If you decide to do this exercise with someone else, first determine who will be the listener and who will be the storyteller. Then assign a specific amount of time for the storyteller to share his or her spiritual history, without interruption or discussion. Remember that the listener's role is to listen and only ask questions for clarification. When finished, thank the person for being a respectful witness and talk about how it felt to be heard. What did you learn about yourself? How has your past influenced your present spiritual beliefs? When ready, switch roles. Then, when you're both finished, feel free to engage in a dialogue about what you've learned.

Continue to write in your journal and don't forget to include the statement for invoking grace to support you as you continue this journey:

> *I am now open and receptive to the power of grace in my life. I ask to be shown clear examples of how I can face this challenge with courage, wisdom, and strength.*

Resources

BOOKS

Addiction to Perfection by Marion Woodman (Inner City Books, 1982)

> *This book explores women's issues, addiction, perfectionism, and the need to control from a Jungian perspective.*

As A Man Thinketh by James Allen (DeVorss & Company, 1979)

> *Building on the Bible verse "As a man thinketh, so he is,"*

just the right times; and reciting the same prayers every week, created in me a sense of devotion and respect for the sacredness of my religion.

When I was nine years old, my interest in religion grew when my parents sent me to Catholic school. Although I would only spend a year there before we moved away, my exposure to daily religious practices at such a young, impressionable age, had a lasting effect. In particular, I was captivated by the nuns with their cherubic faces framed in white, floating through the hallways in long black robes. They were regal and mysterious, and by the end of the school year, I decided that someday, I too would be a nun.

My love of religion manifested itself in unusual ways for a girl my age. During a time when most of my friends hung pictures of TV stars or rock bands on their walls, I hung a tapestry of the Sacred Heart of Jesus, which was given to me by my grandmother. As strange as it may have seemed to others, I felt a deep connection to His image. Every night before going to bed, I would kneel and pray in front of this tapestry. In my young mind, I was firmly convinced that Jesus could hear each and every word, which helped me develop what felt like a very real and special relationship with God. I would call upon this memory (and relationship) later in life as my concept of God and religion changed to reflect more of the woman I had become.

In my late teens, however, I started to lose interest in the church. My inquisitive teenage mind was becoming more aware of the meaning behind the church's teachings and I began to question the message. The weekly services also left me feeling bored and spiritually deprived. There was no *engagement*. Instead, the constant reminder that I was a sinner who needed to be an obedient "God-fearing" church member did the opposite of what it was meant to do. It pushed me away. I *did* learn to fear God and I would grow to resent this later on.

The innocent little girl who once felt comforted by the rituals of the church was now becoming a young woman who felt conflicted by its rules. So, much to my parents' dismay, at seventeen I made a decision to stop attending church. The tapestry of Christ was replaced with the rock and roll poster of the month, and during the time I previously spent praying I started to listen to music, or talk with friends on the phone. I became a religious refugee.

Now, in my late twenties, prompted by the coincidences that were occurring in my life and in the lives of those around me, my interest in spiritual matters had reawakened. In some ways, my Al-Anon meetings had become a substitute for attending church. Because the foundation of the program was spiritual in nature, and because we were encouraged to honor our own understanding of a Higher Power, I felt free to explore a new relationship with God. This, combined with my work in therapy, set the stage for the next chapter of my life.

OPENING TO THE SACRED DIMENSION OF LIFE

Our psychological healing sets the stage for our spiritual growth. As we develop a stronger relationship with ourselves, our confidence and self-esteem increase and the ego defenses that have kept us stuck start to break down. This makes it easier to stop trying to control the world around us, and instead, to allow a higher spiritual source to take the reins. A new kind of awakening begins. The more conscious and open-minded we become, the more likely we are to invite in, and benefit from, the power of grace. Like a Divine tap on the shoulder, a Higher Power gently begins to summon our attention.

During a ride to work, my friend Karen had an experience that illustrates this connection in a clear and direct way: "I remember the day when I realized things were different. *I* was different. I had a conversation with my sister about seeing a therapist to deal with the unresolved anger I had toward my ex-husband. The next morning, while on my way to work, I started getting signs that confirmed the importance of taking this step. While stopped in traffic, I noticed that a car in front of me had a "Let Peace Begin with You" bumper sticker. I stared at the bumper sticker for quite some time thinking, "What if that message is for me? What if it's been put in front of me for a reason?" Then, when the traffic started moving, I switched on the radio to a favorite talk station at the exact moment that the host of the show (normally a funny, controversial guy) started talking about seeing a therapist to deal with his unresolved rage. For the next five minutes he described how his anger had affected his life. When he finished, I turned off the radio, took a deep breath, and let it out slowly. This kind of thing was happening more and more and I was beginning to consider that I was, in fact, getting messages from an other-worldly source."

Once you become open to the idea that coincidences may be a form of Divine communication, you'll start to see them everywhere, and sometimes in places you don't expect. Let's look at a few examples of what I mean.

Grace at Work

When I decided to become a professional speaker, I was anxious to find ways to develop my skills. About a week after I started pursuing opportunities to speak, a friend introduced me to the director of a career networking organization. When the director found out that I was a former tax consultant who'd developed an extensive network of contacts, he asked me to give a talk about relationship building to his group. The timing of his request amazed me. As it turned out, this one invitation led to more than thirty others, giving me the chance to sharpen my public speaking skills.

My client Ryan also had an unexpected turn of events related to his work. He had been working on a consulting project with a corporate client for more than a year. He loved his work and enjoyed the people but, one Monday morning, after arriving at his client's office, Ryan was surprised to discover that the company decided to wrap up the project much earlier than planned. That afternoon, he left his office feeling frustrated and unsettled. But two weeks later, he received a new assignment that took his work to a whole new level. "Had I still been working for my original client, I would never have had the space in my schedule for this great, new opportunity." Ryan added, "They say everything happens for a reason, and in this case, I was surprised and delighted to find that it was for a *good* reason."

Grace in Relationships

My client Derek had a grace-inspired revelation in the middle of an argument with his girlfriend. From the moment it occurred, he knew that his relationships with women would never be the same. Derek had a history of dating women who were critical and emotionally abusive. Each time he'd begin a new relationship, he'd tell himself that he would not allow himself to be treated poorly again.

One night during an argument, while Derek listened to his girlfriend complain about his numerous shortcomings, he suddenly heard a voice in his head that said, "This isn't about me. It's about her. She's putting me down because she feels badly about herself." Derek then looked at his girlfriend and smiled. "I stood there knowing that her behavior had to do with *her* insecurity about our relationship and from that moment on I felt empowered and in control. I could tell by the look on her face that she knew she had pushed me too far. And then, as she began to backtrack, trying desperately to make amends, it became even clearer to me that the relationship wouldn't work. I would never be fooled again. I realized at that moment that I hadn't respected myself enough to attract the type of woman who would respect me. I'm sure it was no coincidence that two months after this happened, I met my future wife."

I had a striking example of how grace intervened on my behalf while dealing with another challenging relationship. After I ended things with my fiancé and spent some time on my own, I entered into a new relationship. Although in many respects this relationship was healthier than the one with my ex, it still presented some major challenges. Eventually I learned that our values weren't aligned and I found myself attempting to fall in love with my new partner's potential. Rather than face the truth and move on, I kept trying to make the relationship work. I was seduced by the dream of what *could* be and blind to the reality of what was.

Although there were many times that I tried to end the relationship, I kept getting pulled back in. We'd make up; start dating again, come up against our differences, and break up. Finally, after I ended it for good, I was starting to get my life back on track. I'd been away from him for almost six months and I was feeling pretty secure—no regrets, no bad feelings, and no doubts about whether I made the right decision. Then I had a moment of weakness.

I'll never forget the day. It was a Thursday in October, early in the evening, and I was on my way out to dinner with a girlfriend. As I was getting ready, I started feeling sorry for myself. For the first time in months, I missed my old boyfriend and thought about calling him. Then, I put the thought out of my mind and continued to get ready.

Just before leaving my apartment, I turned on the television to catch the end of the news. When I did, I saw a commercial for a local show that would be aired later that evening. The topic was "How to Meet Mr. or Miss Right." Since I was thinking about dating again, I decided to tape the show. I picked up a videotape, put it into the machine, and set it to record. Then I left to meet my friend for dinner.

Arriving home at about 11 PM, I felt a bit melancholy. After a night of watching couples share what seemed like romantic conversations in the restaurant, I was left with an

aching sense of sadness. Having no plans for the upcoming weekend, once again, I thought of my old boyfriend and considered checking in just to say hello. Looking back, I can see that this was a normal reaction to the reality that, on a deeper level, I was preparing to let him go for good. I'm sure it prompted my sudden desire to reconnect just one more time. Thankfully I turned on the television instead.

While getting ready for bed, I suddenly remembered the videotape. I went to my living room and turned on the VCR. The host of the singles show appeared and explained that they were going to talk about personal ads. She started by asking the question, "Have you ever wondered what it's like to place a personal ad, or better yet, respond to one? Well, we decided to find out by answering an ad in *Boston* magazine. Here's how the ad reads." She then proceeded to read an ad from a divorced dad.

"We contacted Brad," she continued, "and he's going to tell you what he's looking for." I stood frozen in front of the television, shocked by what I saw. There, in front of my eyes, was my former boyfriend, talking about *his* ad. The host continued. "We decided to fix Brad up with Diane and follow them on their first date. Stay tuned to see what happens!" I immediately hit stop on the VCR, sat back on the sofa, and tried to catch my breath. I couldn't believe my eyes. One moment I was missing my ex and wanting to reconnect, and the next, I was sitting in my living room about to watch him on a date with another woman!

Over the next several minutes, I watched Brad being interviewed by the host about what he was looking for in a woman. He explained that he wanted someone who was upbeat, attractive, and fun. Then, his next comment turned

out to be *my* gift. He said, "I'm looking for a woman who will bring out the best in me." From my point of view, this one statement summed up one of the biggest challenges in our relationship. During arguments, I often heard about how *I* wasn't good enough to bring out *his* best. Brad wanted me to do for him what I believed he could only do for himself.

Something about seeing him on the tape gave me the objectivity I needed to hear his message loud and clear. So thankfully, I never called him that night. Instead, I was sheltered by a remarkable intercession that helped shut the door to that period of my life forever. While this example may sound extraordinary (it still does to me), it was just more confirmation that there was a Divine hand guiding my life.

It's important to note that I wasn't the only one protected that night. Brad was too. Had I not watched the show, I might have called him and rekindled a fire that needed to be put out for good. Calling him wouldn't have served either one of us.

Grace as Protection

Sometimes grace can protect us, as was the case for my girlfriend Max. She had just moved into a new home, and while unpacking came across a set of glass prayer beads, which she placed on top of her stove. Later that day, while setting up the kitchen, Max mistakenly moved the "self-clean" button on the oven to the "on" position. That night while she slept, the oven began to heat up. Unfortunately, the paperwork for the new stove was inside, and there was an empty box on top.

The next morning, Max noticed the smell of something burning. She rushed to the kitchen, checked the oven, and found that it had been on during the night. When she opened the oven door she noticed that the paperwork inside was completely incinerated. The box on the top of the oven was burned as well, but the fire had stopped right at the point where the box touched the beads. Max was convinced that she had been saved by an act of grace.

My client Olivia had an experience of protection when making a down payment on a new home. She met with a real estate agent and began to look at condos in her community. Shortly after, she found one that she liked and decided to move forward with the purchase. She made an offer, which was accepted, and prepared to close the deal.

During the financing process, she met with a mortgage broker—a young man from her hometown. When they sat down and began going through the application, he noticed the location of her condo. He mentioned that he had heard about a water problem in that part of town, and that the issue would become public within the next ninety days. As it turned out, correcting the problem would have cost Olivia over two thousand dollars—money she wouldn't have once the purchase was completed. Receiving this information *before* she bought the condo was quite a break. Olivia backed out of the deal and happily searched for another new home.

Gaining a New Perspective

Sometimes the influence of grace offers us a new perspective that shifts our beliefs or way of being in the world. This was the case for me during a cross-country flight to California. Having survived a horrible flight with my parents in my early twenties, I was a nervous flyer (to say the least). Back then, our plane hit severe turbulence and dropped several hundred feet. Everyone on board began screaming, and I can still remember praying out loud, convinced that the plane was going down.

Several years later I was on another flight, reading a copy of Harold Kushner's book *Who Needs God.* Suddenly the plane hit bumpy air. I continued reading, breathing slowly to try and relax. But soon after, the turbulence got worse and the plane began rocking back and forth. The memory of my earlier flight kicked in and I started to panic. I began to pray, asking repeatedly for God to intervene and stop the turbulence so I could avoid a full-blown panic attack. But it only got worse. That's when I started bargaining.

I began to recite every prayer I could remember from my childhood in the hopes of purchasing my emotional freedom. I was terrified and on the verge of being sick. The turbulence continued. After several minutes, I gave up praying and resigned myself to the fact that I just might die (the ultimate form of surrender). I picked up my book and started reading in an attempt to distract myself from my fear. It was at this moment that I was blessed by the comfort of grace.

At the exact point where I had left off in the book, Kushner began to describe the kind of relationship most people have with God. He suggested that many of us treat God like Santa Claus, asking for favors or to be relieved from hardship and pain. Instead of asking God to remove our painful circumstances, he recommended that we pray for the courage and spiritual fortitude to deal with them.

As I read his words, I instantly felt calmer. A wave of peace washed over me, and in spite of the turbulence, I started to relax. Then I refocused my prayers. I quietly asked for the courage to withstand the rough ride regardless of how long it lasted. It worked. Although the flight continued to be bumpy, I arrived at my destination with my emotional well-being intact.

Besides being an experience of grace, this incident provided one of my earliest lessons on the link between surrendering and receiving divine support. Kushner's advice also spurred a critical shift in my relationship with a Higher Power. To this day, whenever I catch myself equating God with Santa, I remind myself to pray for something far more powerful—the courage and patience to hang in there while my faith is being restored.

My client Ethan, the president of a large marketing firm, experienced an act of grace that changed the way he behaved with his employees. Ethan was working late in his office responding to e-mail, when he came across a message that was mistakenly forwarded to him by one of his managers. It was from a woman who was angry about the way he handled a problem during a meeting that afternoon. She forgot to remove Ethan's name from the CC list.

In her e-mail, she explained that she was offended by the fact that Ethan often criticized other employees when they were not present in the room. She said that his behavior made her feel unsafe and unable to trust his leadership. Her last line made the issue clear. "If he speaks about everyone else that way, I know he must speak about me that way, too."

Receiving this e-mail provided Ethan with important

information about how his actions affected employees. Fortunately he was able to address the issue in a mature and responsible way. He protected the manager by not mentioning the e-mail and immediately stopped being so critical of others. It's interesting to note that the woman who mistakenly sent the e-mail (and other employees) were the recipients of grace as well.

SEEING YOUR PAST THROUGH THE LENS OF GRACE

The more I witnessed the effects of grace in my own life, the more I was able to see it touching the lives of my clients, friends, and family members. I started to wonder. If grace was working in my life now, had it been there all along? Did the fact that I had been sleepwalking through life early on, prevent me from seeing the incidents and messages that had the potential to be gifts of grace? I decided to find out.

I rummaged through my basement and found my old journals. Then I spent several days going through them looking for clues. Sure enough, I could see that things I had forgotten about or taken for granted were much more important, in retrospect, than I had ever imagined. For example, I could see that being the oldest of seven children set me up to be the leader and community builder I am today. In fact, I have many fond memories of bringing my sisters and brothers (and their friends) together to work on projects or to be part of a make-believe school. I loved growing up in a large family and grew to deeply appreciate the camaraderie and support that came from having a common bond.

My family also taught me important personal skills that

would serve me later in life. My father's strong convictions and debating skills, taught me the value of being well informed and able to think on my feet. This helped give me the confidence to teach and coach people in front of large groups. My mother's empathy and compassion for all living things instilled in me a deep respect for life. This inspired my desire to help people improve *their* lives. And finally, living with eight very different personalities helped me hone my negotiating skills. It also helped me to see and appreciate all sides of an issue, teaching me the importance of withholding judgment and being respectful of differing points of view.

In the context of seeing important events in my life as acts of grace, even things I used to view as negative or disappointing were now making sense. For example, for years I regretted not going to college when I finished high school. Funds were limited and at that time it was common practice to reserve college for the boys who would eventually need to support their families. Looking back, I can see that this missed opportunity was actually a blessing in disguise. It allowed me to join my father's tax consulting business at the age of seventeen, and it bred in me an entrepreneurial spirit that still burns brightly today. In addition, I learned how to build a business from the ground up, deal with the natural ups and downs of the growth cycle, and practice taking risks early in life.

When I eventually decided to leave the family business, I suffered through a frustrating period of not knowing what I wanted to do next. For three years I struggled to find something I felt passionate about, not having any idea that the struggle itself—the anguish of not having a clear sense of direction—would actually lead me to the work I'm doing today. During this time I felt embarrassed about not having a secure career, especially since all my friends seemed to be fairly established in theirs. I put enormous pressure on myself to *be* somebody. I longed for a title like lawyer, doctor, or teacher so I could lay claim to a legitimate profession. Like so many people who struggle with career issues, I thought a good job would give me a sense of value and worth as a human being. Even as I write this, I feel such empathy for those who are struggling with this challenge right now in their lives. I know how frustrating and uncomfortable it can be to feel as though you've not yet found your calling in the world.

The pain and suffering I experienced during this stage of my life gave me valuable insight into ways to help people who struggle with career-related issues. Time and again, I would smile inside as I heard myself say to a client or audience member, "Feeling vital and fulfilled has far more to do with who you become on the inside than what you do on the outside." From my current perspective I can see that what we wrestle with in our own lives may actually be training for how we'll be of service to others later on.

My friend Suzie's story provides a powerful example of this idea. It also shows how sometimes our greatest challenges lay the groundwork for sharing our greatest gifts with the world.

"The first person to inspire my life's work was my maternal grandfather, Walter. Walter was stricken with polio when he was ten years old. But, although he was physically challenged, it didn't stop him from living his life to the fullest. When he finished high school, he went on to study at Harvard University and later became a lawyer. Eventually, he would become a judge in the state of Maine. My grandfather never let his disability stop him from doing what he wanted. He taught me that anyone could use adversity to his or her advantage. In fact, I didn't see him as disabled. I saw him as differently abled. He led a very successful life and was an inspiration to me.

"My mother was also ill for many years when I was young. So, for eight straight years (starting when I was eight years old), I shouldered a lot of responsibility at home. My dad was a pilot and would often be gone for five or six days at a time. Although we had a part-time nanny, I still spent a good deal of time providing my mother with the day-to-day care she required. This taught me to have great compassion and sensitivity for people who are disabled or seriously ill. It also gave me the ability to be resilient and resourceful when dealing with setbacks.

"When it came time to choose a college major, my experience with my mother and grandfather inspired me to choose human services with an emphasis on caring for special populations. Since then, I've worked in hospitals, rehabilitation centers, and community needs programs, as well as with handicapped children in elementary schools. I absolutely loved my work and have always felt passionate about caring for children with special needs.

"At the age of thirty-five, I suddenly understood why my life had played out the way it did. I gave birth to my first child, a baby boy named Curtis, who was born with a number of severe handicaps. Not once did I ever ask, Why me God? Instead, I believed I was chosen to care for this amazing little soul. Caring for Curtis is extremely hard work and frightening at times. Yet, I feel honored to be his mother and I know that I've helped him to live a good life. And considering all the times that Curtis has had surgery to correct life-threatening problems, he is lucky to be alive. His doctors say that he might not have lived very long if I wasn't his mom.

"Curtis is now eleven years old. He is functioning quite well considering his many handicaps, which has allowed me to reenter the workforce. I am now working at an elementary school with special needs children and am fortunate to have the formal training and experience to offer them the very best care. And since some of these children come from homes where they don't receive the love and assistance they need, I'm thrilled to be able to spend six hours a day with them telling them how special they are. What's also great is that I have the perspective of being a parent who has faced this challenge herself. I feel strongly that the next step in my journey is to teach and encourage parents to see and treat their children as the incredible gifts they truly are."

YOUR EVIDENCE OF GRACE

Have you ever considered that events that were painful, disappointing, or unfair may have occurred to nudge, or perhaps even *shove* you in a more positive direction? Are there themes or patterns that seem to be trying to get your attention? Your life contains evidence of grace, and you'll see it if you take the opportunity to look at your past in a new way. The experiment at the end of this chapter is designed to help you do just that. By reviewing your life and answering the questions, you'll begin to see that your life is perfectly orchestrated by a benevolent, organizing force that supports your emotional and spiritual growth.

Today, I'm convinced that everything does in fact happen for a reason and that we're constantly being presented with opportunities to evolve to new levels of wisdom and understanding. The evidence I found in my past experiences confirmed this for me. But the most powerful evidence of all came from looking at my relationships. When we learn to see the people in our lives for who they really are, we see that they are guiding lights in a sense promoting and encouraging the development of our souls. Hopefully, after completing the next phase of this journey, you'll never look at another human being the same way ever again.

———◆———

While finishing up this chapter on finding evidence of grace, I decided to take a break and go for a mountain bike ride with my friend Susan. When our ride was finished and we headed home, we talked about the magic of nature. "I wonder if there really are such things as nature spirits or gnomes," Susan said. "Sometimes, when I'm riding in the forest, I feel some kind of magical presence." As I considered her idea, I was reminded of a book I read long ago by a woman who traveled to Ireland to research the history of leprechauns. She came back from her trip convinced that they were real.

As we continued our ride home, I started to tell Susan about the book. Just then, a truck pulled out in front of us. We quickly came to a stop and watched it turn. Susan and I looked at each other with surprise and delight. The name on the side of the truck read, *The Shamrock Paving Company.* "What if the universe really is that magical?" I chuckled. I believe it is.

Experiment: Re-Viewing Your Past

Now it's your turn to play detective by searching for clues that mark the influence of grace in *your* life.

Set aside at least a half hour for this exercise. Then, with journal in hand, imagine that you could rise above your life and look down on your past from a higher perspective. Think about how certain events or experiences may have supported your spiritual evolution. Write down anything that comes to mind. Next, choose at least one question from the following list and use it as a guide for writing in your journal.

- In what ways was living with your family the perfect springboard for the life you live today?
- What major challenges have you faced? How were they blessings in disguise? What did they teach you about yourself, life, or others?
- Were there any difficult periods that prepared you to be of service to others? If so, how?
- Are there any themes or patterns that have steered you in a particular direction?
- How have the painful events of your past served you in a positive way?

Once you've finished this exercise, mark this page (or pages) in your journal so you can review your answers, particularly when you need encouragement or a boost of faith.

Also, write the following statement in your journal so you continue to invoke grace:

I am open and receptive to the power of grace in my life now. I ask to be shown clear examples of how this energy is operating in my life.

Resources

BOOKS

Many Lives, Many Masters by Brian L. Weiss (Fireside Books, 1988)

Based on a true case history, this book explores the healing power of past life therapy. Regardless of your beliefs, the message in this book will change forever the way you look at death.

The Spontaneous Fulfillment of Desire: Harnessing the Infinite Power of Coincidence by Deepak Chopra (Harmony Books, 2003)

A glimpse of how seemingly coincidences are dramatically meaningful to our everyday lives and the power we hold within.

Who Needs God by Harold Kushner (Fireside Books, 2002)

An insightful book in which Rabbi Kushner addresses the need for spiritual commitment in our daily lives.

MAGAZINES

Science of Mind

This monthly magazine offers great articles on a variety of spiritual topics.

4

WHO ARE YOUR SPIRITUAL
CHANGE AGENTS?

IMAGINE MEETING A CAST of characters at the beginning of your life who agree to take on roles that will assist you with your spiritual development. Some agree to take a leading role like a close friend, family member, or spouse. Others might play a supporting role—a doctor, a financial advisor, or a therapist. There are characters who will support you through thick and thin, and those who will challenge you in difficult ways—a betrayer, an angry parent, or a disabled child. In this chapter, you'll have a chance to see these characters for who they really are—spiritual change agents— people who raise our consciousness in some way and, as a result, support our spiritual progress. When you review your past and present relationships from this perspective, you'll develop a whole new understanding of how the people you come in contact with serve an important purpose.

"God speaks to us through people," is a phrase many of us have heard at one time or another, but few of us ever recognize how true it really is. When we set out to look for evidence of grace, we soon find it in the interactions we have with others. Sometimes it's during a brief exchange with a person who delivers a piece of wisdom that makes us look at the world, or ourselves in a different way. Other times it might be through an on-going relationship with a person who challenges us to acknowledge an unhealthy habit, or shortcoming we've been unable to admit. And then there are people who, through their unyielding love and support, leave an indelible mark on our hearts, giving us the strength and encouragement we need to stay true to our souls.

When I considered my past relationships, it became apparent that many of them involved people who were clearly spiritual change agents. Like actors in a divinely inspired play, these change agents played both major and minor roles in the drama, and at times, comedy, called my life. They helped shape my character, nurture my spiritual development, and challenge me to respect and express my God-given talents, in spite of my fear, self-doubt, and inability to see clearly where I was headed. Sometimes their roles were obvious. For example, my first therapist was the loving and compassionate partner I needed to begin my healing process. And, the boyfriend who wanted me to bring out his best was a catalyst for learning to respect my personal needs. In hindsight, I can also see that some people played far more important roles than I realized at the time.

In 1991, my friend Lucy was diagnosed with terminal cancer. She was eighty years old and had lived a full life. She was a brave woman with a fiery spirit—a tough cookie who never minced words. On the day of her diagnosis, I went to visit her in the hospital. Like a reporter delivering the evening news, she quickly informed me that she didn't have long to live and asked if I would be willing to help get her affairs in order. I was totally taken aback. At this point in my life, I had not had a close experience with death and my initial reaction was a firm "No!" The thought of supporting someone who was dying terrified me. It was far too intimate.

Lucy was a widow and had no children. In addition, she didn't have an extended family and the guilt I felt at the idea of leaving her to die alone took precedence over my fear, so I agreed to her request. I'm so glad I did. Over the next three months, Lucy and I spent many hours together talking about life, her experiences as a world traveler, and the regrets she had at not having done the things she really wanted to do. Our time together was a once-in-a-lifetime experience, and the more we talked openly about death, the less I feared the dying process.

It wasn't until after Lucy died that I realized what a wonderful gift it was to witness the completion of her life. In some ways she played the role of a spiritual sage, by helping me see the importance of not having regrets and by giving me a firsthand experience of what really matters at the end of our lives. Lucy also held a firm belief in an afterlife and her faith did much to help lessen my fear of death. She helped me to see the end of life as merely a transition from a physical existence to a more spiritual one.

Some special people come into our lives and leave us with important wisdom about living. Take a moment to reflect on your past and the people who've taught you your most important life lessons. For example, maybe you learned how to live more in the moment while playing with your young son. Or, maybe you found the courage to pursue your love of acting because of the encouragement you received from your eleventh-grade teacher. Think about the messages you received about life from your mother, father, or a grandparent—messages you've taken most to heart and remembered all these years. Spiritual change agents, whether they are five years old or fifty, are always trying to help us see life from a more enlightened perspective. The trick is to pay attention.

ANGELS IN TIMES OF GREAT NEED

According to my friend Katie, her spiritual change agent—what she called a just-in-time ally—helped her come to terms with her father's death. As Katie's father entered the last stages of his life, she became extremely depressed, more so than she'd ever been before. When her father died, Katie could barely function. She was having a tough time keeping up at work, and when she was home, she spent most of her time in bed. She became so depressed, in fact, that she worried that she would lose her job.

Katie was a member of a women's group—a group of seven colleagues who'd been meeting for over two years. One evening, a woman from her group called to discuss their next meeting. Hearing something strange in Katie's voice, Sandra gently asked her if she was okay. This simple act of caring brought tears to Katie's eyes and gave her an opportunity to mention her father's death. A few minutes into the conversation Katie broke down and told Sandra the truth—she was severely depressed and didn't know what to do. Within thirty minutes Sandra was at her front door with a cup of tea, a box of Kleenex, and the name of a psychologist who specialized in grief counseling. Unbeknownst to Katie, Sandra had lost her own father just one year before.

When Katie resisted the idea of counseling, Sandra asked why. "I don't know. I wouldn't know what to say. How would I find the right one? What would I ask?" It was then that Sandra took matters into her own hands. She grabbed a notepad and started writing down questions for Katie to ask when she made her calls. Then, Sandra picked up the phone, dialed the number of her psychologist and waited as Katie left a message. Much to their surprise, the therapist called back within fifteen minutes.

Looking back on that experience, Katie could see that Sandra led her to the perfect resource. As it turned out, Katie required medication to relieve her depression. It was unlikely that she would have recovered so soon without Sandra's intervention. Sandra's kindness and prompt response allowed Katie to use her father's death as a catalyst for change. "I will be forever grateful to Sandra for giving me the support and resources I needed to heal and get my life back. I know I'm a much better woman today for having made the choice to use my dad's death as a means to live a more conscious life."

When I hear about stories like Katie's, I'm reminded of how one small act of kindness can have powerful results. Not only did Katie get the help she needed to deal with such a painful loss, she got it almost immediately. I've seen this happen quite often. When a client is in a tough place and needs support, the power of his or her emotional state opens the heart, and this opening attracts the help that is needed.

It's when we're in a receptive state that we can see, and respond to, the light of grace. As a result, we often experience dramatic evidence of how a Higher Power is protecting and directing our lives. Of course, the idea is to learn how to attract this support without needing a crisis to open your eyes. You'll learn how to do this in the next chapter.

A GIFT IN DISGUISE

Sometimes the people who have the most powerful effect on our lives are the ones who cause us the most pain. I certainly saw this early in my relationship with my fiancé. While the last year of our relationship involved a lot of struggle and suffering, this experience enabled me to awaken and do what I needed to heal. And our relationship led me to Kelly, the friend who introduced me to Al-Anon. Kelly's role at that time in my life was that of a guardian angel. She opened the door to an emotional and spiritual awakening that led me to where I am today.

In 1993, after being introduced to the emerging profession of coaching, I entered a relationship that had a profound effect on the direction of my life—the relationship I shared with my first coach and mentor, Thomas Leonard. Thomas was a brilliant man, a prolific creator, and a person who was deeply committed to providing the tools and resources people needed to live extraordinary lives. He single-handedly launched the profession of coaching in 1992 and set the stage for thousands of people to get the support they needed to change their lives.

Thomas challenged me to commit to becoming the best coach in the business. He encouraged me to always tell the truth, set firm boundaries, and practice what he called extreme self-care. Because of his coaching, I was able to create a strong foundation of emotional and physical health, financial reserves, and high-quality relationships. My practice flourished, and eventually I was able to fulfill my dream of writing and publishing books. Thomas's mentoring not only had a dramatic effect on my life and me, but also on the lives of the individuals I touched with my work.

Like many mentoring relationships however, ours became strained over time as I developed greater independence. Thomas was a skilled communicator and had very strong opinions. His directness could be intimidating, and when we disagreed, I often backed down even when I didn't share his views. Eventually our relationship hit a wall when we found ourselves on opposite sides of a professional decision that needed to be made together. When I finally stood my ground and expressed my unwillingness to do things his way, it was clear that our partnership was over.

Although I was deeply saddened by the loss of this relationship, our disagreement taught me an important lesson about standing my ground and honoring my integrity, in spite of the conflict I knew I might face. I also learned a critical lesson about relationships. Sometimes the most loving thing we can do for one another is to let the relationship end. My experience with Thomas helped me understand that there will be people who come into our lives for a specific purpose, and when that purpose is fulfilled, it may be necessary for everyone's sake, to move on.

Drina, a workshop participant, shared a painful experience that turned out to be an encounter with a spiritual change agent. During the workshop, I asked for volunteers to discuss a specific situation where they felt the need to stand up for themselves. Drina raised her hand and said that she had recently been passed up for a promotion at work. "The position was given to a younger, less-qualified woman. I feel unappreciated and ripped off. I need help with how to tell my boss how angry I am."

Listening closely, I watched as Drina expressed her anger and frustration. When she finished, I took special note of her last remark. "I guess I just have to realize that people are always going to rip you off at one time or another." This last statement held the clue to the promise of grace.

"Do you realize that your last statement may reflect a belief that is affecting your life in a negative way?" I responded. Drina gave me a puzzled look. I continued. "The phrase 'people are always going to rip you off' represents the kind of expectation that often gets fulfilled, especially when we have a lot of emotional energy behind it. Your beliefs become the rules you live by. Because of this, they actually have the potential to draw these experiences toward you."

As Drina considered this idea, she looked at me with a blank expression, so I asked her to try an experiment. I had her close her eyes and take a few deep breaths to get centered. Once she felt more relaxed, I asked her to think about another time in her life when she felt ripped off. She immediately responded. "All my life. Hasn't everyone?" I quickly asked for a show of hands from those who agreed with Drina. Nobody raised their hands. I then asked Drina to scan the room, and as she did, a look of surprise crept across her face.

In an effort to reframe Drina's present-day experience of having been ripped off, I suggested that this one event might, in fact, be linked to others in her past. If she was willing to explore the roots of this belief, she might be able to change it and recognize the grace in her present situation. Immediately Drina said, "Wow, I just had a flash of insight. I can hear my mother's voice in my head warning me about being ripped off by people. I think this memory may have something to do with it." This is where grace came in.

As Drina considered the message she received from her mom, she realized that it dated back to an early childhood event when her mother was clearly upset about having been betrayed by someone. She didn't know the exact details, but she remembered her mother using strong language to describe how she'd been ripped off. Once she uncovered the root cause of her belief, I wanted her to see how it had played out in her life. "Drina, take a moment to look back over your life for evidence of being ripped off and tell me what you notice." After careful thought, she identified several instances when she felt taken advantage of or short-changed in some way.

With this new perspective, I suggested that although she was entitled to feel angry with her boss for giving the job to someone else, his decision might have been a gift of grace. After all, it brought her to this moment and allowed her to realize how much she'd been influenced by her erroneous belief. I then asked Drina, "Is it possible for you to see your boss as a healer, someone who was placed in your life to help you mend this old wound?" As Drina considered this idea, she began to cry. Someone who seemed like such an adversary just a short while ago had now become a catalyst for a whole new perspective on life.

As painful as they may be, some of our most difficult relationships hold the promise of our greatest healing. When you learn to see your relationships in this way, you might discover that the friend who constantly took advantage of you, did so (on a spiritual level), to challenge you to stick up for yourself. Or the family member who betrayed you (after you ignored the gut feeling that told you something wasn't right) may have done so to teach you to trust your intuition.

As much as our adversarial relationships can offer powerful insights that dramatically alter the way we view our lives, we are equally influenced by those who stand by us and believe in us when we have difficulty believing in ourselves. These types of spiritual change agents often play a pivotal role in the direction our lives take. *How* we meet them can be a miracle in and of itself. There were two meetings in particular that will always amaze me. One involved my love life, and the other involved my books.

MEETING A TRUE SOULMATE

In 1993 I was living alone in a small apartment near Boston and for the first time in many years I was content and happy. My speaking business was growing, my health was good, and I was enjoying time with my family and friends. The only thing missing was a partner. Although I'd been dating a little, I was still tentative about the idea of starting a new relationship. I didn't want the drama that I experienced in my past with other men. Yet as time went on, I realized that to have any chance of the kind of relationship I'd always wanted, I would have to confront my fear. So, to get the process rolling, I started writing about the kind of person I wanted to meet. I allowed myself to imagine a best-case scenario by describing the physical, emotional, spiritual, and intellectual qualities that would depict my ideal partner. By the time I finished, I had created what I called an ideal partner profile, an exercise I would use time and again with clients later in my work as a coach.

Several weeks later, on a Saturday night, I sat in my living room talking with my girlfriend Julie. Julie was a talented improvisational actress, and in the middle of a discussion about meeting a partner, she picked up a magazine from my living room coffee table and, just for fun, began reading the personal ads that were listed in the back. I laughed as I listened to her—with different accents—read ads from men who were seeking partners. Then, Julie handed me the magazine and told me to give it a try. I started looking through the ads to find a suitable character and immediately zeroed in on one particular ad. "Wow," I said. "This one actually sounds pretty good!" I read it out loud.

Knowing how lonely I'd been (and tired of hearing me complain), Julie suggested that I call and leave a message. "No way," I said. "I would never respond to a personal ad. It's too risky and I'm much too shy to do something like that. Besides, I'm not that desperate." Julie gently pressured me at first, but it was when she dared me that I picked up the phone and called the box number in the ad. To my surprise, I was connected to a computerized voice that instructed me to leave a message for box 3452. I quickly hung up. "There's no

voice mail message and I'm not responding to a computer. I knew it was a bad idea. Let's just forget it." Julie shrugged her shoulders and dropped the subject.

The next morning, I noticed the magazine on the coffee table and read the ad again. "Hmm," I thought. "This really is a good ad." Then I put it down. Every day for four days, I picked up that magazine and reread the ad. I was particularly interested in the fact that the ad described his character and personal qualities rather than the kind of woman he desired or a description of an ideal date. So on day five I threw caution to the wind and decided to make the call. Phone in hand, I offered a silent prayer. "Okay," I said, "this is my declaration to the Universe that I am ready, willing, and able to meet a life partner. Whether he calls back or not, please hear this prayer as my willingness to be open to whatever my next step should be." Then, after erasing and rerecording my message at least ten times, I left a short, fairly nondescript invitation for him to call. Then I forgot about it. As far as I was concerned, it was now up to Providence.

Declaring my intentions or asking for what I want *out loud* is something I began doing after a meeting I had with a yogi. During our conversation she made it clear that she was committed to doing God's work and felt comfortable asking directly for what she needed. "I often tell God that if He wants me to follow a certain path, He must help me find it," she said. "I expect help and I *always* get it in some form or another." Her comfort with requesting what she needed was a refreshing departure from what I learned as a child. So I did what she suggested. I too found that when I asked for direction or guidance, I often received an answer.

Two days after I left the message, a man named Michael called back and we set up a time to speak. I was surprised (and a little scared). It was important to me that we talk before deciding to meet because I didn't want to waste my time. There were several questions I wanted to ask to be sure we shared a similar outlook on life. Having invested so much energy in my own personal growth, I knew what I wanted in a relationship—no drinking or drugs, and a man who valued his emotional and physical health. I had no interest in dating an unconscious guy.

When we finally talked on the phone, Michael patiently and graciously put up with my interrogation. He answered each of my questions carefully and thoughtfully. Then he began asking *me* questions. He wanted to know about my past relationships—why they didn't work and what I had learned about myself in relation to men. He was interested in my thoughts about children, marriage, and counseling if a couple got into trouble. Michael was also interested in the kind of personal work I had done to prepare for a committed relationship. I was surprised and impressed by his directness and willingness to engage in what I considered a very honest and sensitive conversation. At the end of our two-hour call, we agreed to meet for dinner.

On the night that I met Michael, I knew immediately that he was special. He was warm, funny, and refreshingly honest about who he was and what he wanted out of life. During the course of our conversation, I asked him why he placed a personal ad. His response held a clue to what I now see as our Divine connection. Michael explained that in the past he often played a passive role when dating, and as a result, found himself dating women who expressed an

interest in him rather than proactively searching for women he wanted to get to know. "I placed the ad as a statement to myself and to God that I was ready to meet someone special. I had no expectations at all. As far as I was concerned I didn't have to respond to anyone. I just wanted to see what happened." As I listened to Michael talk, I remember thinking, "This is not some ordinary man and this is not some ordinary date!"

Michael and I continued to see each other over the next several weeks, and during this time, I discovered an amazing fact. Michael received more than 150 responses to his ad. He had received letters and photos from models, actresses, and women with similar professional backgrounds. I was the only person he called. When I asked him why he said, "I have no idea. It wasn't that your message was all that compelling. My hand just started dialing the phone. There was no logical reason why I should've called you and no one else."

Every day we receive intuitive nudges, feelings, or messages from what I call our Wise Self. Unfortunately, most of us are too busy to listen or afraid to act on this information. We also tend to over-analyze the messages we receive, spending too much time pondering questions like, "Is this just wishful thinking? Can I really trust this feeling? Should I check in with someone else first?" While it's true that important decisions often require forethought and careful planning, sometimes we need to relax our busy minds and trust our inner voice—our Wise Selves.

As I see it, you can't go wrong by tuning into your Wise Self. Even if you make a choice that doesn't work out, by taking your intuition seriously, you send a message to your

Wise Self that you're paying attention. When you do, the messages get clearer and stronger. Your willingness to listen to, and act on, your feelings and insights will become as valuable, and perhaps even more valuable, than using your logical mind.

Although falling in love at first sight always sounded wonderfully romantic, I never really believed it could be true. But meeting Michael challenged this belief. Our connection *felt* right. Not more than a few weeks into our relationship, I was sure he'd be the man I'd marry. He felt unusually familiar, as though I had known him for a long, long time, and I felt very much at home in his company. One day, while looking through some of my old journals, why I felt this way became even clearer. Here's an excerpt from a journal I finished a year before my first date with Michael:

> *I'm with a friend and we go to a theater. I am introduced to an Indian woman dressed in royal blue and purple clothes. She is with two men. One is Indian and the other is American. I am attracted to the American. He is very handsome, with dark hair, brown eyes, and a very kind smile. He is strong and muscular and his name is Michael. I feel drawn to him, as if we've known each other before.*
>
> *Next, my dream shifts, and I see Michael standing on what looks like the deck of a ship. Actually it's a simple boat without any sides; a flat deck that floats on top of the water. At the head of this boat is a point, much like a long rectangle with a triangle attached to the end. Michael is standing in the center looking out over the water.*

The last line in my journal read: *Is there a Michael looking for me?*

As I sat reading and rereading this entry, several things surprised me. First, the fact that the man was named Michael. Next, the description of his appearance was accurate. Michael was muscular and strong (he'd been working out since he was ten years old), had dark hair, brown eyes, and a very kind smile. Finally, the strangest part of the dream was the boat. Not only had I described the flat bottom that Michael was standing on, I drew a picture of it in my journal with an X to mark the spot where he stood.

Two months after we started dating, Michael took me to the site of a home he was building in the town where he grew up. It was under construction and he wanted to show me the inside. Michael went into the house first while I took my time looking around the yard. Then, when I stepped through the front door, I had to catch my breath. I looked up and saw Michael standing on a balcony. The focal point of this balcony (and the home) was a pointed platform that looked just like the boat I had drawn in my journal. There was no mistaking this scene. It was clearly what I saw in my dream, a year before Michael and I ever met!

THE POWER OF SPIRITUAL PARTNERSHIP

For the last twelve years, both Michael and I have been secure in the knowledge that our meeting was an unmistakable touch of grace. It was obvious to both of us that we were (and are) spiritual change agents in each other's lives. While we've had our disagreements like any other couple, we're both clear that our primary role is to provide each other with fertile ground for living spiritually conscious lives.

When I think about a spouse or a partner as a spiritual change agent, I recall a conversation I had with an old friend many years ago. Eleanor had been happily married for ten years and she felt strongly about how marriage could enhance a person's life. "People who marry are like two beautiful birds who come together to build a sturdy nest. They work hard to create a home that includes love, respect, nurturing, and honesty. Once this sacred space is in place, they each take flight. Both birds are able to make their greatest contributions to the world because they have a secure home and loving partner to return to for spiritual sustenance."

A soulmate is a spiritual change agent who makes a commitment to stand by you as you navigate through life. He or she will remind you of your greatness when you forget, push your buttons so you're inspired to heal, and challenge you to grow. He or she will also support you in staying true to the voice of your soul. It's important to note that a soulmate doesn't have to be a romantic partner. My client Jill considers her best friend Deirdre her soulmate— a spiritual sister who shares her passion for personal and spiritual growth. Jill and Deirdre read the same books, attend retreats and workshops together, and even get together to meditate. "My relationship with Deirdre is just as important to me as my marriage. We share the same values, speak the same language, and challenge each other to live our best possible lives. If it wasn't for her, I wouldn't be where I am today."

MEETING THE MIDWIFE

Another type of spiritual change agent comes into our lives at a pivotal point, usually to mark some kind of transition or significant change. He or she is like a midwife (or mid-husband). A midwife's job is to help us develop and express the talents we're most meant to share, to assist us in transitioning through new phases of our lives, or to encourage us to awaken to the signs and gifts of grace. For example, a midwife may act as a mentor, providing guidance by offering expertise in a new field of interest. At times a coach can take on this role. A coach may help you find your true calling, create a plan of action to pursue it, and hold you accountable as you move toward achieving your goal. A midwife can also support you in birthing a new phase of your life, such as going from employee to business owner, or single career woman to mom. My midwife helped give birth to my writing career. With her love, guidance, and unwavering encouragement, I was able to express my passion for writing and share my message with the world.

◆

By 1996, my coaching practice was in full swing and I was considering the idea of publishing a book. I wanted to write about the process I used with clients to help them improve their lives. To set the wheels in motion, I worked with an experienced magazine writer, developed a pitch for a story about coaching, and submitted it to what was then *New Age* magazine (now *Body & Soul*). My ultimate goal in getting the article in print was to attract a publisher or literary agent who might be interested in my book. Much to my surprise, the magazine quickly accepted the story. It was slated to be a one-page article, but soon turned into a full-length feature story about the emerging field of coaching. When the magazine came out, it not only offered an in-depth look into my work and the work of several colleagues, but also included a full-page, color photo of me in my home.

It's not uncommon to step into the flow once we've partnered with a midwife and opened our lives to grace. As a matter of fact, having things fall into place is a good indication that we're on the right track.

Sure enough, a few weeks after the issue hit the stands I was contacted by a publisher, and three literary agents who all asked if I had considered writing a book. When I said yes, each of them wanted to see a proposal. For the next several months I worked hard to develop an overview, a chapter-by-chapter outline of the book, a sample chapter, and a comprehensive marketing plan.

Six months later, when the proposal was complete, I wasn't sure what to do next. While I knew people were waiting to see my proposal, I had no idea whether or not it was any good. So, rather than send it out sight unseen, I decided that I needed help. First, I needed to know if my idea was cohesive enough for a book. Second, I needed to find out whether my writing was good enough to write a book without a ghostwriter or coauthor. It was time to get some objective feedback, but I didn't know where to go. That's when, once again, I prayed for direction.

"Okay God," I announced, "if I'm meant to write this book I need some help. Please give me a sign, so I know what to do next." Almost immediately a woman's name popped into my head. It was Maggie Lichtenberg. Maggie is a book marketing and writing coach who has a private practice helping writers get their projects off the ground. I immediately picked up the phone to see if she had any ideas.

Maggie answered on the first ring and her response was a good indication that my prayer was received. "It's so funny you should call. I just had lunch with a woman who used to be an editor at a major publishing house and she happened to mention the article in *New Age* magazine. She asked me about you and this new profession called coaching. Why don't you give her a call and see if she might be willing to take a look?" I thanked Maggie for her idea, and as soon as I hung up the phone (before my fear had a chance to set in), I picked it up again and called the editor.

I've come to believe that taking immediate action is another important conduit for receiving the gift of grace. The more time we waste analyzing our moves, considering the negative consequences of our actions, or thinking about our fear, the greater the possibility that we'll interrupt the flow of thoughts, feelings, and ideas that we most want and need to express. Yes, it's important to make key decisions carefully, but when your next step presents itself loudly and clearly, do yourself a favor. Take action before you talk yourself out of something that could bring you, and others, great joy.

After discussing my idea with Marilyn (the editor Maggie suggested I call), she agreed to look at my proposal. Once I knew she was interested, I asked her to tell me a little bit about her experience in publishing. I wanted to be sure that I was sending my writing to someone I could trust. Marilyn explained that she had been the editor-in-chief at a major publishing house, and if that wasn't enough, she had also worked with some of my favorite self-help authors. When I hung up the phone, I sat back in my chair, excited (and anxious) about sending her my proposal. It was clear that I was going to get feedback from one of the best editors in the business. That's grace.

I sent my proposal to Marilyn and waited patiently for her reply. But I wasn't just waiting for feedback about my book; I was waiting for something more. I wanted a professional opinion about whether I had the skills to be a published writer—something I had dreamt about since I was twelve years old. One week later, Marilyn called. I can still remember that my mouth was so dry I had trouble trying to talk with my lips sticking to my teeth. The vulnerability I felt about having a professional read my writing was palpable. Like so many of us who courageously attempt, for the first time, to put our dreams out into the world, I knew that if she criticized my work there was a chance I might abandon the idea of writing a book, and perhaps, never try again.

When I talked to Marilyn, she got right to the point. "Not only can you write," she said, "but you have a good, solid book idea in the making. I'd love to help you polish the proposal so you can submit it to an agent and get this thing published!" I took a deep breath and let out a sigh of relief. I was thrilled. I immediately remembered the twelve-year-old girl who kept a diary so long ago, and the woman who carried on the tradition by using a journal to help transform her life. Having come full circle, I could once again see the influence of grace. I would have an opportunity to fulfill my dream of being a professional writer.

Five years and four books later, I can see that Maggie

was my first spiritual change book agent—a connector who brought Marilyn and me together. Marilyn was, and still is, one of the most important spiritual change agents in my life. A dear friend and colleague, I have no doubt that she was a gift of grace, and a powerful midwife sent to help me share my work with others. Without her, I may have never had the courage to pursue my dream.

There is no doubt that you have come here to share *your* gifts with others too, and I can assure you that there are midwives waiting to support your efforts. Think about it. Who in your life may be able to help you get started on fulfilling an important dream? Is it a coworker, a former boss, or an old friend? Next, expand your thinking *beyond* those close to you. Is there a friend of a friend who might help? An extended family member you haven't seen in a while? Remember that grace often shows up in unexpected places. Keep your eyes and ears open.

GRACE WORKS BOTH WAYS

In both my relationships with Michael and Marilyn, grace worked both ways. Not only were they important to my growth and development, I was important to theirs, as well. Michael had been married once before and seriously questioned the viability of another marriage. His divorce had left him gun-shy, too. Our relationship and subsequent marriage challenged assumptions he made about what he could or couldn't do with his life. Also, Michael, who is generally soft-spoken and reserved, believes that our partnership gave him the confidence to pursue goals he had never considered, such as speaking in front of groups and publishing his own books.

When I first called Marilyn, she had just moved to New Mexico with her husband, Sandy. Both had left high-profile positions at New York publishing houses to spend time traveling throughout the country. She was now getting settled in New Mexico and trying to figure out what she wanted to do next. Marilyn was clear that she wanted to work with people she liked, and on projects that inspired her. But this time, instead of working long hours and being motivated by her earning potential, she wanted to strike more of a balance between doing work that she loved and enjoying a satisfying personal life. As it turned out, work/life balance was the theme of the first project we worked on together. My first book, *Take Time for Your Life,* offered a program that helped readers do exactly what Marilyn wanted to do—find a balance between their personal and professional lives.

As I look back on my life, it's clear that marrying Michael and meeting Marilyn were pivotal events. Michael's honesty and unwavering support provided me with the confidence and solid foundation I needed to fully own and express my talents. Each time I came face to face with my fear of failing, he helped me find the courage to persevere. Marilyn did, too. Like many first-time authors, I would often start out trying to write what I thought readers wanted to hear, or I'd find myself suffering from writer's block, questioning the value of what I had to say. Marilyn kept me focused and wouldn't let me hide my voice. She knew exactly how to move me beyond my fear.

◆

When you think about the significant people in your life, in what ways have they helped you change? How have you helped *them*? How are they serving your personal and spiritual growth? How are you serving theirs?

A CHANCE MEETING

My friend Brian was in his third year of college studying to be a teacher. Toward the end of the year, he discovered that his roommate (who lived with him during his first two years at school), was transferring to another university. Unfortunately, this left him with very little time to find a new roommate for the following year. As Brian considered his options, he opened his date book to a page that had "Gavin," the name of one of his classmates, scrawled across the top. "Hmmm," he thought, "I like Gavin. We have a lot in common. I think he'd be a great roommate. But I'm sure he's already sharing a room with somebody else. So much for that idea."

As Brian made his way to the housing office later that afternoon, to put his name on a list, he ran up a flight of stairs and turned left, suddenly coming face to face with Gavin. Brian blurted out, "Who are you rooming with next year?" "Nobody," Gavin replied, "my roommate is dropping out of school. Do you want to room together?" "Sure," Brian said. "Okay," Gavin replied. And they both went on their way. "Wow," Brian thought, "I can't believe that I ran into Gavin just then. And I can't believe that he wants to share a room with me next year! What an amazing coincidence."

Sometimes a chance meeting, or a spontaneous thought or idea, is an indication that grace is at work. The spontaneous decision Brian and Gavin made to be roommates started a lifelong friendship in which they would become important spiritual change agents in each other's lives. For example, four years after leaving school, Gavin's life hadn't turned out the way he planned. Instead of landing a job in his field of study (health and fitness), he worked with a moving company during the day, and as a part-time bartender at night. Gavin said he spent most of his free time on the phone, in front of the TV, or at a local bar with a few buddies from work. Brian's life, on the other hand, had moved in a more satisfying direction. He was the general manager and fitness director at a prestigious health club in New York.

Brian and Gavin stayed in touch over the years, and one day, Gavin called Brian to catch up. During their conversation it was clear to Brian that Gavin was unhappy. Then, on a whim Brian said, "Gavin, why don't you quit your job, pack your bags, and come to work here at the health center. We're expanding and I'm sure we can find a place for you." And in about the same time it took him to make the decision to be Brian's roommate, Gavin said, "When do I start?"

"That one phone call changed my life," Gavin said years later. "Suddenly, instead of being bored or drunk every night, I was eating well, exercising every day, and getting my act together." Gavin went on to become a physical therapist and has dedicated his life to helping people heal. When I asked Brian what made him invite Gavin to work at the health facility, he said, "It was a spur of the moment thought. I wasn't even sure we had a position available. But it's all worked out for the best. Gavin is the most loyal and supportive friend I've ever had. He's made a big difference in my life, too."

My colleague, Ted, had a surprise encounter with a stranger that offered him the blessing of grace in a moment of panic. "I was leading my first workshop at my church," Ted said. "I thought I was well-prepared, so I decided that I didn't need any notes. The event was to start at 7 PM on a Wednesday night, so I arrived at 6:00 to be sure I had everything I needed. Then, at 6:30, I went into a backroom to do a last-minute rehearsal. Suddenly I began to feel anxious and my mind went completely blank. I was terrified and afraid I'd start the workshop and lose my train of thought. I started to hyperventilate.

"At 6:45 PM I was sweating profusely. I couldn't remember anything—not even the subject of the workshop! Then, there was a knock on the door. A woman appeared out of nowhere and asked if I needed anything. I told her that I was about to begin my first talk and couldn't remember a thing I wanted to say. To my surprise, she immediately dropped her purse, grabbed my hands, and started praying for me. When she finished she said, 'Right before you start your talk I want you to say: God speak through me. Once you say this you'll have nothing to fear.'

"As I slowly made my way to the room where everyone had gathered for the workshop, I kept repeating those words over and over—God speak through me, God speak through me, God speak through me. I continued as I heard myself being introduced. When the introductions were finished, I stood up and looked out over the audience. Suddenly, all the fear left my body and I started to speak with confidence and conviction.

"I said everything I wanted to say and more. The feedback I received was positive and I was asked to speak again.

The woman who helped me reminded me of an angel. In fact, I was so moved by her presence that I wondered if I had imagined her. Did God send her to me at just the right moment? All I know is that I never experienced the same kind of fear again."

What if everyone you meet is a spiritual change agent—a messenger sent to support you in some way? Would knowing this change the way you view the people in your life now? Would you respond any differently to new people you meet?

Every day we receive, and offer others, gifts of grace. Once you see how people are planting seeds for your spiritual growth, either through the support they give you, or the challenges they present, every conversation you have becomes so much more than just an exchange of thoughts or ideas. It becomes a communion of sorts; a sacred event that, in some way big or small, has the power to change you forever.

———•———

Now that you've seen evidence of a Higher Power in both the events and relationships that have shaped your life, you're ready to learn how to partner with this energy to live a more soul-directed life. You're ready for the next lesson; learning how to dance with grace.

Experiment: Meet Your Spiritual Change Agents

This experiment is designed to help you identify your spiritual change agents and understand what they're meant to teach you. Consider your answers carefully as you complete the following steps:

1. Regardless of how well or long you knew them, choose one person from your past who influenced your life in a positive way. Write the name in your journal.
2. Now choose one person from your past who was negative or adversarial in some way. Write the name in your journal.
3. Choose two people from the present—one who is influencing your life in a positive way and one who is adversarial and write their names in your journal, too.
4. One by one, hold each person in mind, write his or her name at the top of a page in your journal, and answer the following questions:
   a. If you had to assign a role to this person, what role would you give him or her? Catalyst? Messenger? Challenger? Midwife? Soulmate? Angel? Teacher? What other roles can you think of?
   b. Now imagine this person came into your life to give you some kind of gift. What might the gift be? A life lesson? A piece of understanding or insight? The motivation to make a change?
   c. What one piece of wisdom could you take from this relationship that would serve you in moving forward with your life?

The next part of this experiment is intended to deepen your relationships with those people who are sharing your journey now. Schedule a time to sit and talk with someone with whom you are close, for example, a trusted friend, coworker, or family member. Then, take turns asking each other the following questions:

- What contribution has our relationship made to your life?
- What role do you see me playing in your life? (catalyst, messenger, teacher, angel)
- How have I been a teacher?
- How have I challenged you to grow?
- How have I introduced you to a new way of looking at the world?

When you are finished, compare notes. Are there any similarities? Any surprises? Talk about how you both might deepen your relationship based on the information you've received. How will each of you become a more conscious spiritual change agent in each other's life?

Resources

BOOKS

Dare to Forgive by Dr. Edward Hallowell (Health Communications, 2004)
> *This book provides an honest and loving look at the path to forgiveness.*

Only Love Is Real: A Story of Soulmates Reunited by Brian L. Weiss (Warner Books, 1997)
> *An endearing love story of soulmates in the afterlife.*

WEBSITES

www.cherylrichardson.com
> *You can find or start a Life Makeover Group in your community by using our free online database.*

www.eharmony.com

> *One of the most successful online dating communities, it uses extensive scientific matching technology to help people find partners who share their values.*

www.Meetup.org

> *A website designed to help people get together with a group of neighbors who share a common interest.*

www.spiritualcinemacircle.com

> *A terrific subscription community that provides monthly movies with a spiritual or compassionate message not ordinarily seen in theaters.*

5

◆

DANCE WITH GRACE

I'm standing in a grand ballroom in the center of an old stone castle. There's an orchestra playing classical music at the front of the room. Out of nowhere, an Asian man with a warm smile approaches and invites me to dance. As we start to move, he says that he's going to teach me the dance of life.

"See yourself dancing effortlessly," he explains. "Trust me to lead." "Relax and surrender to the music. Be patient as you learn." And finally, "Take pleasure in the dance."

I do my best to follow his lead. Soon, we are gliding across the floor, as if floating above the ground. I am totally in the moment, unencumbered by limitations of time, space, or physical matter. As we move in unison with the music, I realize that I am receiving a rare glimpse of the creative process. I surrender and become entranced by the flow of the dance. I awake feeling hopeful about my future.

This dream served as a metaphor for the next stage of my journey—a stage we all reach when we invest in our personal growth and become more open to seeing and respond-

ing to grace. It's a period in life when we stop blaming people or external circumstances for the quality of our lives, and
we take back our power. Instead of seeing things happening
"to us," we start to understand the role we play in making
them happen.

The years of hard work on myself and my life were paying off. Now that I had improved my health, and achieved
emotional and financial stability, I was excited about my
future. I had finally settled into my work as a coach and I
was enjoying the process of helping clients change their
lives, too. During this time, my approach to life began to
shift. I became a proactive and responsive partner to the
signs and messages that showed up in my life. I trusted my
gut and had faith that a Higher Power was always available
to point me in the right direction. I only needed to pay attention and act. In a sense, I was beginning to dance with grace.

In this chapter I'd like to offer you a process for learning
how to dance with grace, too. Here are the four main
lessons you'll be invited to learn:

Lesson 1—Understand the Basic Choreography

Lesson 2—Partner with a Higher Power

Lesson 3—Surrender to the Music

Lesson 4—Trust in Divine Timing

LESSON 1 – UNDERSTAND THE
BASIC CHOREOGRAPHY

Prior to the launch of my coaching, speaking, and writing
career, I learned a fundamental lesson about the nature of
life—what I came to see as the basic choreography of how
things work. I learned how to use my mind to produce and

direct my life instead of passively watching it unfold. I achieved a greater understanding of this principle from reading spiritual classics that offered great insight into the basic laws of creation. The first was *The Power of Constructive Thinking* by Emmet Fox, published in the early 1930s. In this book he proposed that we all have the ability to cocreate our lives with God, and the key to doing so is to harness the power of the mind. For example, in one chapter Fox suggests using a simple technique called spiritual treatment to correct a specific problem. In essence, a treatment consists of intensely focused prayer, turning your thoughts away from the problem, and thinking only of God and the desired outcome. The idea is to spiritualize the problem by shifting the focus of your mind away from the constant thoughts of worry and dismay, to something far more powerful—a Higher Power.

Fox's teaching reflected the basic laws of metaphysics—using the power of the mind to create physical reality. In today's world it can be quite a challenge to direct the mind. We are so often fueled by adrenaline and anxiety that we end up living in a constant state of fight or flight. This creates anxious neural pathways that make focusing on worries or problems a default position for the mind. Learning to control your thoughts by consciously overriding conditioned negativity is an important step in creating a self-directed life.

I put Fox's advice to use immediately. For example, every time I started worrying about my future or finding my true calling, I replaced my anxious thoughts with affirmations that "a Higher Power is directing my life." Then, because I tend to be very visual, I created a mental picture of myself looking happy and satisfied while doing work I loved. As soon as I became aware of any fearful thoughts, I would immediately shift my focus to the inner picture I had created, making it brighter, bigger, more vivid, and alive. I also imagined that I was creating a new neural pathway—a fresh, healthy groove in my mind that would eventually reverse my tendency to focus on the problem.

My introduction to Fox's work increased my interest in other spiritual books that echoed his metaphysical views about the power of the mind. It was then that I began to read *The Dynamic Laws of Prosperity* by Catherine Ponder. Her book offers specific examples of how people were able to create abundance by using affirmations to reprogram old, self-destructive thoughts. For example, after considering Ponder's advice, instead of focusing on the low balance in my checkbook each time I balanced my bank statement (a habit that left me feeling vulnerable and powerless), I focused on the way that my life was rich and abundant already. Every month, before balancing my statement, I would list twenty things I was thankful for (on the actual statement itself). This little ritual helped me to keep a positive attitude while I worked to improve my financial health. I also kept a gratitude list on my desk, to which I would add anything I could think of that influenced my life in a positive way. Gratitude is such a powerful notion—a force of energy that draws good into our lives. These actions helped me to stay focused on what I wanted rather than what I didn't have.

When we take a proactive role in directing our thoughts and words toward the outcomes we most desire, we begin to get our first glimpse of what it's like to ignite grace. For example, when I focused on abundance it was not unusual for me to receive an unexpected check, or to have a bill come in with an amount due that was for less than I expected. Once again, harnessing the power of your mind is the key; and the best way to do this, I've found, is to take the time to make a specific, strategic plan for your life. Although there are many ways to do this (and many books available on the subject) I like to keep things simple. I believe that the best place to start is by taking the following steps—the first lesson of the dance. They are:

- *Set Goals*—Move from passive reaction to proactive intention
- *Adopt New Beliefs*—Act like you have arrived
- *Trust Your Gut*—Learn to listen to yourself first
- *Get into Action*—Move from dreaming to doing

Taking these actions is the first step to leading your life on *your* terms. Instead of leaving things to chance, you need to identify what you want and go after it. Then, once you've set your goals, you can improve your chances of achieving them by taking your lead from someone who has already accomplished them. The next step is tuning into your inner voice—using your internal compass to determine the best way to steer your ship. Finally, you need to act.

When it comes to creating your best possible life it really is this simple: decide what you want, shift your beliefs, trust your gut, and act. Now let's look at each step in more detail.

Set Goals

When I first decided that I wanted to have more control over what happened in my life, I set new goals in eight

areas—physical, emotional, spiritual, financial, intellectual, professional, material, and fun. At first I challenged myself to consider every possible option—a difficult task if you're not used to allowing yourself to want more than you need. Because I was a thrifty thinker, I had to challenge myself to consider goals that seemed impractical or far-fetched.

I believe that we all have a set point—a level of success that we feel worthy of or comfortable with. For this reason, when you consider what you want in life, it's important to think outside of your comfort box—to imagine things you've never believed you could achieve. It's perfectly fine to consider things that seem over the top, or out of the realm of possibility. Since you're learning to design your own lifescape, you'll want to train yourself to expect (and accept) the best. I can assure you that some of the most outrageous goals I ever set, the ones that never in a million years could I have imagined coming true, were goals that I not only achieved, but exceeded! So, don't let your past determine your future. Raise your set point by allowing yourself to think big!

Adopt New Beliefs

Once I had a long list of goals, I reexamined it to decide which ones would be my top priority. After choosing one goal from each category, I thought about how I would have to adjust my beliefs to support my pursuit of each goal. To facilitate this, I identified people who were already successful at creating what I wanted. Then, I asked them about the specific beliefs they thought had served them best. For example, one of my goals was to get out of debt. I felt so

overwhelmed by my unpaid credit card balances that I spent a lot of time focusing on how bad things were. Instead of listening to my old, self-defeating beliefs such as, "I'll never make enough money to pay off my debt," or "It will take forever to be debt free," I focused on creating new beliefs indicative of those someone would have if already debt free.

My colleague Wendy was a wonderful role model as I worked to improve my financial health. She had no debt, made good money at her job, and invested it wisely. I asked her to share the beliefs that best supported her ability to eliminate her debt. Her reply was very helpful. "Living without debt gives me the freedom and power to live my life the way I want. To me, paying off debt is like making an *investment* in my financial health." As I listened to her, I wrote down two new beliefs: "Being debt free = power and freedom," and "Paying off debt is money in the bank." I affirmed these beliefs repeatedly, from that point on. Whenever I had any fear about money, I would repeat these statements. They became my wealth-building mantras.

Trust Your Gut

Once I began replacing old beliefs with new ones, it became even more important to use my intuition to determine my next steps. After years of listening to everyone else, I was finally learning to listen to myself. This is a very important point. Too often, especially when we're first learning to take control of our lives, we doubt ourselves and we tend to seek advice and direction from others. Then, when we do what they suggest and it doesn't pan out, we wonder what *we* did

wrong. Over the years I've found that putting too much stock in someone else's view of what you should do is a sure way to *prevent* grace-inspired insights. The Divine energy that is available to each and every one of us is ready to support the highest plan for *your* life, not the life someone else believes you should live. While it's helpful to get input from those we respect, it's far more important to develop a strong connection with your own inner guidance system, especially in the early stages of learning to cocreate your life with the Divine.

As I continued creating my plan of action, I quieted my mind and waited for a sign or sudden insight about what to do next. Should I contact a particular person, read a certain book, or send a letter? My good friend Bruce says "the language of grace is intuition," and it was becoming clear to me that there was a direct connection between my willingness to listen to and follow my inner wisdom, and being able to stay in the flow. It wasn't until I got in the habit of checking in with my gut and trusting it enough to act, that I consistently found myself moving in the right direction.

Over the years I've heard many stories from people that underscore the link between grace and intuition. Sometimes the message we're meant to get is almost impossible to miss. For example, Patricia, a retreat participant, said that when she was shopping for a new home she kept hearing, "Find the yellow house. Find the yellow house." Then, after looking at several homes that did not suit her needs, she was finally taken to a yellow house. Patricia said, "I knew immediately that it was the house I should buy. And, once I made an offer on it, it only took five days for my old home to sell. What was even more amazing was that it sold for the exact price I needed to be able to purchase my new home."

Sometimes, even when the timing seems wrong, we may need to trust that our intuition knows something we don't. For example, when Edna, a woman from our online community, paid attention to her inner voice, she found herself attending college and fulfilling a lifelong dream of becoming a nurse. Edna got her message one night while walking on a treadmill. She said, "I was strolling along thinking about the fact that I never pursued a career in nursing, even though it felt like an important dream. I had thought about it a lot, but the idea of returning to school to complete my degree scared me to death. I wasn't sure I could do it."

Now, in the middle of her workout, Edna felt compelled to take action. She got off the treadmill and went into her office to log on to her computer. Trusting this inner nudge, she immediately began surfing the web and found a state college just a short distance from her home. Besides offering the specific program she was seeking, the school had an application process that could be completed online. Edna took immediate action and submitted an application. Only two weeks after filling it out, Edna received an acceptance letter. Shortly after, she began taking courses and was on her way to becoming a nurse.

Our willingness to take our intuition seriously gives us a greater awareness of how grace is influencing our life. And eventually, it makes our lives easier. When Edna and I talked about the night she applied to school, she told me that the process seemed *too* simple. She couldn't imagine that something she wanted so much could happen so quickly and easily. I've heard this quite often. Experience has taught me that trusting our intuition is one of the most powerful ways there is to become aligned with our Divine plan. When we're tuned in, spiritually and energetically, it's not uncommon for things to fall into place. Regardless, there's a natural tendency to resist or question the ease with which things happen. We're so trained to believe that we must struggle or work hard to achieve our goals. But, when we learn to listen to and act on our inner wisdom we often find a quicker and simpler path. In fact, oftentimes it's the simplicity itself that signals an act of Divine intercession.

Get into Action

Once you've adjusted your beliefs, used your intuition, and developed an action plan, you're ready to act. Start by asking for help. It's time to ask your role model—the person who has already achieved what you desire—how he or she made it happen.

When I asked Wendy how she became debt free, I was so inspired by her story that I quickly followed her lead. "I made a list of all of my debts," she said, "and hung it on the wall in my office. Then, I thought of the debt elimination process as a game. First, I set up a minimum payment schedule. Then, I used any extra money I earned to pay off the debts with the highest interest rates. My next step was to update the list at the end of the month (after I paid my bills) and celebrate every time I decreased my balance. Sometimes I would celebrate with a friend, while other times I simply did something fun on my own. Although I didn't realize it at the time, I was training myself to associate joy with declining balances. Within fourteen months my debt was completely paid off!"

During our discussion, Wendy also mentioned how surprised she was that things seemed to happen so easily. "Once I made a commitment to eliminate my debt I could hardly believe what happened. A friend invited me to attend a professional luncheon where the topic was women and money, and I learned that I could call my credit card companies and renegotiate high interest rates. As a result, I was able to get the percentage on two credit cards cut *in half.* Then, for the first time since joining my company, I was allowed to work extra hours, so I applied my overtime pay to the outstanding balances. I also remember getting some great advice from a guy I met on a train. It turned out that he was a financial planner. I spent the whole ride getting a private consultation on the best ways to get out of debt!"

Looking back, I can see that Wendy provided the inspiration and practical advice I needed to activate the power of grace in my own life. Within one year after I followed her advice, my debt was completely paid off.

Once I set a goal, identified and adopted the appropriate beliefs, and trusted my gut to move me in the right direction, I took additional steps to ensure my success. Every night, before I went to sleep, I made a point to visualize myself accomplishing all of my goals. I also made signs on which I wrote each new belief and goal, and hung them up throughout my house. They served as visual reminders to keep my mind focused in a positive direction. While I'm sure my apartment must have looked strange to friends, I didn't care. As far as I was concerned I was conducting metaphysical research, and these tools were helping me take charge of my most important asset—the creative power of my mind.

The practice of these four basic steps forms the foundation of a more spiritually mature perspective on life. As you take back your power from the external world, your level of consciousness expands and from this higher perspective you are no longer able to see yourself as a victim. Instead, you gradually realize that *you* are the architect of your life. Your thoughts, your beliefs, and your actions play a vital role in what happens to you. And, once you fully comprehend this universal truth, you're ready for the next lesson:

LESSON 2 – PARTNER WITH A HIGHER POWER

By this time, I had faith that a Divine power was guiding my life. While I knew I had free will and the ability to direct the course of my life with my thoughts, I also believed there was a greater spiritual force influencing my future. I was ready for a more intimate relationship with this power—or what I now felt comfortable calling God.

To create a stronger connection with the Divine I did a number of different things. To begin, I gave God a human face making the concept of a Higher Power easier to relate to. I often spoke to this image as I went about my day asking for what I needed—the energy to continue my work, or the clarity to see a problem from a clearer or healthier perspective. In addition, I shared my gratitude. I was constantly saying, "Thank you, God" for the beauty I saw in nature, the gift of a restful night's sleep, or for the rich conversation I shared with someone I loved. Sometimes I would even write to God in my journal, venting about a challenging situation, asking for guidance, or expressing my feelings about the changes occurring in my life.

When it came to my career, I began to think of God as my business partner. If there were important decisions to be made, I would sit quietly and ask for the wisdom to make the right one. Instead of seeking praise, financial success, or notoriety, I did my best to make serving others the focus of my work. When I needed help, I came to expect the support I needed. For example, the day before I was about to give a speech to over eight hundred people, I lost my voice. When I reached the door of the auditorium, I said, "Okay God, if you want me to do this, I could use some help. Please give me a voice!" Sure enough, as soon as I was introduced, my voice came back and I was able to give the talk. Then, the moment I walked out of the building, my voice was gone.

And, of course, I prayed. In the morning, before going to bed, many times throughout the day. I also prayed before writing and, always, before giving a speech. I asked to be used as a vehicle for the exact type of insight or guidance people needed to overcome an obstacle or to make an important change. I can see now that I was reestablishing the kind of partnership with a Higher Power that I had as a young girl. But, this time, I wanted a more mature connection, something different than what I had before, which was God as a judge to be feared and me as an unworthy sinner.

My connection to a power greater than myself also led me to understand the concept of flow. Each time I asked for guidance I learned to pay close attention to the flow of energy that resulted from my actions, remembering my dream of floating effortlessly across the dance floor. If something was repeatedly a struggle and doors seemed to keep closing, I assumed it meant that I should go in a different direction. When a door opened quickly and easily, I assumed it was for a good reason and moved toward it. When a direction *felt* right but didn't lead where I wanted or expected, I waited patiently for my next step to be revealed. As I learned to trust the messages I was getting, it wasn't uncommon to end up in an entirely unexpected place.

My colleague Sean developed a ritual that helped strengthen his relationship with a Higher Power. He said, "In the morning I make myself a cup of coffee, sit down at the kitchen table, and open a notebook that I keep on a nearby shelf. Then, I write the same question at the top of the page: 'What should I do with my life today?' Then, I wait patiently until I feel moved to answer. I'm not comfortable using the word God, but I do believe in a Universal Spirit and I believe that it helps me answer this question."

Sean explained that he would write down anything that came to mind, regardless of how random or unimportant it seemed. The message might be: "slow down, call your sister, get to work early, meditate, or reorganize your office." As he continued this ritual, he learned to have more faith in it and more often than not, found that the answers he was getting led to some very important decisions regarding his health, career, relationships, and lifestyle. On days when he'd wake up late and rush to work without taking time to write, he would often feel restless and off balance. Sean also noticed that taking time to tune in with a Higher Power made him better able to accept circumstances he couldn't control. This allowed him to have more compassion for himself and the people in his life.

My client Lainey, a devout Christian, uses prayer to talk directly to God. She spends time in the morning and before she goes to bed, talking to Jesus about her day. "I ask for His blessing," she says, "and the courage to do His will. In the evening I review my day and run through a list of everything I feel grateful for. I thank Him for blessing my family and ask for guidance in areas where I feel stuck, lost, or out of control."

My friend Bonny says she feels a strong connection to the feminine aspect of God and has established a relationship with an Indian woman, Ammachi, who is regarded by many to be an incarnation of the Divine Mother. Ammachi is often referred to as the hugging saint and in India, where she is most well known, she often hugs thousands of people in one sitting. Bonny had an opportunity to listen to Ammachi's teaching (and get a hug) during one of her visits to the United States. Bonny said, "The moment Ammachi touched me I felt an overwhelming sense of love. Her energy was beautiful and I knew in my heart that I wanted to study her teachings. I've been able to build a relationship with the Divine Mother through Ammachi and it has given my life meaning and a clear sense of direction."

How we go about establishing a relationship with a Higher Power is a personal choice that each one of us makes in our own way, in our own time. It's not enough to attend a church or temple, pray for assistance only in times of need, or study spiritual books. As human beings, we need to feel a real, tangible connection. In fact, a survey of our online community showed that a stronger relationship with a Higher Power was among the top desires shared by our members. The way to develop a partnership with a Higher

Power is to engage in activities that strengthen and nurture the relationship—activities that open up the lines of communication. With this kind of ongoing connection in place, you're ready for the next dance lesson.

LESSON 3 — SURRENDER TO THE MUSIC

The ability to surrender is a sign of spiritual maturity. It's a skill that requires patience and practice. Whether we're faced with a fear of loss, anxiety about an uncertain outcome, or the aching desire for something we can't have, our willingness to relinquish control and put faith in an outcome we cannot yet see is a crucial element in learning to dance with grace. The challenge is learning to surrender *before* the suffering begins.

When I think about my life, I can see that when I'm able to surrender my will to a Higher Power, things are no longer a struggle. Life gets easier. Fear melts away and I feel more at peace. I have faith that I can handle any situation in a way that supports my highest good. I no longer waste enormous amounts of energy trying to maintain an illusion of control. Instead, I find that when I slow down, and take my hands off the wheel, a power greater than myself seems to take hold to steer me where I need to go.

Our source of suffering is always related to our resistance to what is. The soul doesn't try to control life, the ego does. When your ego is wrapped firmly around a desire, your peace of mind and happiness are held hostage by an obsessive need to control the outcome. After enough pain and suffering, you'll eventually get the message: If you don't learn to surrender your will, you *will* surrender your peace.

It takes a leap of faith to abandon *your* way for the *right* way. It means letting go of how you think things *should be* and accepting them as they are. When we surrender, it doesn't mean that we simply throw our hands in the air and do nothing at all, it means that we pay close attention to the messages we get from our Divine partner so we can act on this wisdom. Then, once we've done what we can, we let go and allow the Divine to take over to bring about the result that will serve our spiritual development.

Here's another thing you should know about surrendering: it doesn't just mean placing your trust in the unknown. It also means facing the reality that you may not get what you want. It took a long time for me to see that like so many of us, when I struggle and suffer, it's often an attempt to control a situation in order to avoid disappointment. But the reality is that we will be disappointed at various times throughout our lives. As we practice the art of surrender, however, we allow grace to shine a light on a better path.

The idea of letting go and allowing the right way to reveal itself became clearer to me after being interviewed about coaching for a feature story in a national magazine. Before the story was published, I was informed that my part of the interview would not be included in the piece even though I had spent several hours answering questions. The writer explained that she was taking the story in a different direction.

When I received the news I was extremely disappointed. Every time I thought about the interview I'd get upset all over again. I went back and forth in my mind, trying to find a way to reintroduce my work to her so that she could find a better fit for her story. Finally, when I got tired of agonizing over it, I let it go. I told myself that there must be a reason for the change that I didn't yet understand and I stopped obsessing about it.

When the article finally appeared, I discovered that I was right. The angle that the story took would have reflected poorly on me and my work. As I sat in my office with the article in hand, I felt both embarrassed and relieved. Rather than doing harm, the writer actually helped protect my reputation. I also learned an important lesson about letting go. Things often work out for the best in ways that we can't imagine or don't expect.

"If you could suddenly rise above your life and look behind the scenes you'd understand why things happen the way they do. But you can't. Sometimes you just have to surrender." This little piece of wisdom came from a woman I met during a conference. She was speaking from experience. Noreen was away with her family on vacation when she received some terrible news—just short of her sixtieth birthday, her mom had a stroke and died. "On the six-hour flight to join my family," Noreen said, "I prayed for the strength to stay composed. It was the longest flight of my life. Then, during both the funeral and week of sitting Shiva, I found myself struggling to come to terms with my mother's death. I felt tortured about not being there when she died and not having one last chance to tell her how much she meant to me. I finally faced the reality that there was nothing I could do to change what happened, except surrender and let my emotions run their course. There is something about grieving that teaches you what it really means to let go. In the depth of my pain, surrender was often my only course of action."

Learning to surrender doesn't require a long, drawn out series of painfully difficult steps. A simple prayer like, "Help me to accept the things I can't change," can go a long way toward helping you let something go. Let your prayer be an invitation to grace, one that says, "I'll trust my intuition, take the steps that feel right, and do my best to release my attachment to the result." Surround yourself with reminders that will inspire you to let things go. For example, I have two signs that hang on the wall in my office. One says, "Surrender Draws Grace,"(a phrase I mentioned earlier from my friend Jerry), and "The World Is Conspiring in Your Favor," (compliments of my friend Bruce). Every time I see these signs I'm reminded to trust and let things unfold as they may.

How would your life change if you were as good at surrendering as you are at trying to be in control? Think about it. What are you trying to control in your life right now? What do you need to do differently to let it go? For example, instead of badgering your son about cleaning his room, why not make your expectations (and consequences of not doing it) clear, and then allow him to find his own way. Or, instead of arguing with your wife, you could let go of your need to be right and focus on reaching a compromise. When you surrender, you make space for miracles to happen.

LESSON 4—TRUST DIVINE TIMING

The final dance lesson can be the toughest one of all— patience. Once we've learned how to harvest the creative power of our minds, partner with a Higher Power, and surrender the outcome of our actions, we're ready for the next step; learning to trust that our lives will unfold in the way, and pace, that is best. This means putting your trust in Divine timing—developing the patience to hang in there while the world conspires in *your* favor.

The publication of my first book taught me an important lesson about Divine timing. Prior to a book being released, the publisher creates a game plan, or a publicity strategy, to generate sales. Executing this plan can (and usually does) result in a good deal of disappointment. There are radio interviews that get bumped because of late-breaking news, newspaper stories that never run, and television bookings that fall through at the very last minute. It can be extremely discouraging (especially for new authors) who are excited about the potential for success. I was no exception. Early in my career I experienced a major setback that, in time, turned out to be a huge blessing in disguise.

As the publicity efforts for my first book ramped up, I received the call that every aspiring author hopes to get. *The Oprah Winfrey Show* invited me to be a guest. Needless to say I was thrilled and imagined how this would help me reach a wider audience and advance my career. To my surprise, though, the week before I was to appear, I received disappointing news. The show didn't need me after all. They decided to use someone else.

Like so many authors who dream of appearing on the show but never get the chance, I was extremely disappointed. This was one more blow in a string of disappointments and I was beginning to think that my skin wasn't thick enough to handle the stress of dealing with the media, a prerequisite to being a successful author. It took a few months to lick my wounds, get centered, and carry on with my work. During this time I taught workshops, made appearances on local radio and TV stations, and coached people during live presentations. Then, about one year later, the Oprah Show called again. This time I exercised caution as we went about planning the show. Finally, when the day came for me to appear as the featured guest, everything went without a hitch—so well, in fact, that they asked me back. A string of subsequent appearances turned into a yearlong feature called "The Lifestyle Makeover Series," an outcome I never could have imagined.

The timing of my first show was critical to the success I experienced. By then, I knew what women wanted, and I had the confidence and experience to speak about it on television. Had I been on a year earlier, I wouldn't have had the experience and media savvy to do one show effectively let alone carry a whole series. The lesson was clear: There's our timing and then there's Divine timing. Place your bets on the latter.

If you think about it, I'm sure you can remember times when you wanted something right away but were forced to be patient, much to your dismay. This happened to my client Isabel while conducting a job search. At first, things seemed to be going well; people were responding to her networking inquiries, she had had several interviews, and she felt confident and secure that she'd find a position soon. Then she interviewed for a job with a telecommunications company, a job she was desperate to land.

Two weeks after her interview, Isabel still hadn't heard from the company and she was getting impatient. "I felt totally out of control," she said. "The longer I went without hearing from them, the more desperate I became. I ended up leaving the manager six voice mail messages but never heard back."

Isabel wasn't offered the position. As a result she became even more aggressive in her job search. "From that point on," she said, "I stopped getting calls for interviews and new job leads seemed to dry up."

One day a close friend gently suggested that her desperate, controlling behavior might be not only preventing her from attracting new opportunities, but actually repelling them. After hearing this Isabel said, "I'm so grateful that my friend had the courage to tell me the truth. My fear had gotten the best of me. So I reassessed my behavior, adjusted my attitude, and let things unfold as they were meant to, without expectations. Sure enough, within a few days I received two great leads, both for positions I was well qualified for. One month later, I had a new job with a company I really liked."

When things don't fall into place in the timeframe you expect, use it as an opportunity to practice patience. Remind yourself that it's probably for a good reason. Write the following phrase on a piece of paper and keep it in your wallet: *"Haste will take the place of something better born from grace."* When you're feeling frustrated, take it out and read it. In my experience, the most exciting and/or beneficial opportunities have *always* taken more time than I would have expected. And, they've always been worth the wait.

STEPPING ON TOES

Dancing with grace isn't like doing the perfect waltz. You *will* get tripped up at times. Anticipating obstacles (and paying attention) will keep you on your feet. In addition to the barriers we've covered already—taking a passive role in your life, dancing without a strong partner, trying to control the outcome, and being impatient—there are other blocks to watch out for. These blocks include putting more stock in what others think instead of trusting yourself; procrastinating about the things that matter most to your soul; and continuing to do the same old thing time and again, even when it's not working.

Sometimes we retreat from grace by retreating from others. As a matter of fact, isolation can be a covert form of control. By assuming that we're the only one who can solve a problem, or that others won't be there for us, we delude ourselves into thinking we're in charge. But we seldom are. Typically, the more we isolate the more frightened and anxious we become. And, fear and anxiety interrupt the flow of grace.

Focusing on the Downbeat

Negative thinking can also prevent us from experiencing grace. When you focus on beliefs like I never get what I want, or life is too hard, you place a wall between you and grace. While, at times, we all fall prey to bad moods and negative thinking, it's important to be mindful of how powerful our thoughts really are. My client Logan admitted, "Focusing on what I was afraid of or didn't want to happen seemed to draw toward me the very thing I hoped to avoid. For example, whenever I'd start to save money, I'd worry about getting an unexpected bill in the mail. Sure enough, nine times out of ten, that's exactly what happened. The more committed I was to identifying and releasing my negative thoughts, the more receptive I was to the power of grace."

Tripping Over Stuff

According to my friend Connor, what kept him from experiencing grace was having too much *stuff*. Once he decided to clean up his life, he was forced to address his reluctance to let things go. The amount of clutter in his home and office was preventing him from moving forward. It wasn't until he acknowledged this that he made the connection between too much clutter and being walled off from grace.

Connor reminisced, "I had so much junk around my home that I could barely see my rooms! Whenever I needed something like a book or tool, I had to wade through two feet of clutter just to get anywhere near it. Fortunately, cleaning up my life was the catalyst that helped me awaken to grace.

"As I made my way through each room in my home, I was amazed by what I found. I couldn't believe I had saved so much junk! Each time I threw something out I imagined that I was letting go of old stuff that was keeping me stuck. And, over time, as my home became less and less cluttered, I noticed that I had more space for new friends, experiences, and opportunities. I can't tell you how many times letting go of a box of old books or files led to a new business opportunity or new friendship. Decluttering my home was a yearlong process that completely changed my life. I got so used to being rewarded when I let go of things that held old energy that it became a kind of game."

Connor went on to share a specific example of this principle in action. "As I became convinced that a Higher Power was guiding my steps, I started to relax and trust that even the most challenging situations would work themselves out over time. And they always did. For example, at one point my wife and I decided to buy some investment property. We researched multifamily homes in our area and discovered that there were very few in our price range. We were also told by our realtor that based on the current market, we'd be unlikely to find one for quite a while.

"That weekend I thought a lot about what we needed to let go of to make space for a new property. It occurred to me that I had some very expensive diving equipment in my garage that I had been trying to sell for more than three years. Unfortunately, I couldn't find someone who would pay me enough to feel good about letting it go. So, I hung onto it. But each time I went into the garage, I was reminded of the equipment. Not only did it represent something I was no longer interested in, it screamed, 'bad investment!' So, that afternoon I went through the phone book and found a search and rescue organization that could use the stuff. I packed up the equipment and loaded it in the back of my truck. It was a tough decision. The gear was worth well over $3,000. But, when I donated it, the crew was so appreciative of the unexpected gift that I left feeling good about my decision.

"Then, twenty-four hours later, not one, but two investment properties, owned by the same person, came on the market. Not only that, the seller was willing to hold a portion of the mortgage to make a quick sale. My wife and I made an offer immediately and bought both properties! I don't know how or why it works but for some reason, whenever I let go of old things, better things come into my life."

WHO'S LEADING THE DANCE?

My ability to dance with grace generated a lot of changes in my life. Over the next four years I would publish three books, appear on numerous television and radio shows, and travel around the country teaching people the practical strategies I had used to restore sanity to my own crazy life. At the same time I was engaged in this outer work, I continued to be diligent about my inner work—staying grounded, raising my level of integrity, and using every experience as an opportunity to become a more conscious human being. Toward the middle of 2001 I was getting tired of traveling. The cost of success was steep, and I wasn't sure I wanted to pay the price. Living out of a suitcase and spending night after night in a hotel wasn't as glamorous as I imagined. Eating mediocre food, breathing stale air, and rushing from one event to the next were taking its toll on my emotional and physical health. One day, I knew I was in trouble when I caught myself looking for a seatbelt as I sat down in a theater to watch a film with my husband. I forgot I was at the movies and thought I was on a plane!

Being a private person, suddenly faced with a public life, was also quite a challenge. I wasn't used to the kind of attention that being on television brings. On one hand I was deeply grateful for the opportunities that were being presented to me, and on the other, I felt unsettled. I struggled with questions like, How do I deal with the fact that so many people around me assume I've changed? How do I welcome this abundance without becoming too attached to it? Am I prepared to deal with the loss of my privacy? The biggest challenge of all was the isolation I felt in considering these questions. I had no close friends or confidants who had dealt with these issues. Also, I didn't want to be seen as ungrateful. It was a strange dichotomy; I was on such an incredible high while at the same time questioning whether it was what I wanted.

As much as I wanted to believe that I could balance this kind of success with a sane and fulfilling personal life, I knew better. I couldn't admit it at the time, but I can see now that I needed space to reevaluate my direction. The conflict I was experiencing was reflected by my increasing struggle to make things happen, something I'd always been good at doing. When our actions are in conflict with our values, we lose power and it becomes difficult to move forward. During a conversation with a good friend, I shared my frustration about things not falling into place the way they once did. He offered me some sage advice: "When what you've always done stops working, it's simply an indication that a shift is about to occur. A new phase of your life is trying to emerge. Let it be born."

While I had no idea what this something new was, it was clear that my ambivalence about the cost of success was making it more difficult to hold a steady vision of what I thought I wanted to achieve. I felt pulled in opposite directions. For example, I wanted to reach large numbers of people with my message, yet I didn't want to live in airports and hotels. It was gratifying to have my books on the *New York Times* bestseller list, and yet I didn't want the pressure of having to produce a new book every year. I was grateful to be able to share my message on talk shows and news programs, but I didn't know how to be a public person with a private life. Right about the time that I stopped denying that something needed to change, I had a profound experience that was a striking example of grace.

———◆———

The morning was sunny and bright. I was en route to Boston's Logan Airport where I was meeting my best friend Max. She was joining me on a business trip that included a stop in California to deliver a keynote speech at a conference, and then on to Arizona to present a workshop at my favorite spa Miraval Life in Balance. When my work was done, Max and I planned to spend a few days together getting massages and relaxing in the sun. It was September 11, 2001.

When I arrived at the airport I went straight to the American Airlines gate where I was supposed to meet Max. I was so excited about our trip, especially since it was the first time we would travel together across the country. As I sat at the gate waiting for Max, I started to get nervous. Passengers were about to board the plane and she still hadn't arrived. When I heard the boarding call, I grabbed my bag and headed down the jetway. Then, my cell phone rang. It was Max letting me know that she was stuck in traffic. "If I miss the flight," she said, "don't worry. I'll take the next one out." It was about 8:30 AM and our plane was scheduled to depart at 9:15.

As the passengers boarded the plane I chatted with one of the flight attendants. I told her about my friend who was running late and jokingly said that I wished the flight would be delayed so she could make it to the airport. A short time later, the flight attendant returned and informed me that she had good news: our flight would be delayed by fifteen minutes. I relaxed, feeling more hopeful that Max would make the flight. Then my cell phone rang again.

This time it was my mother-in-law Pat. Normally a very calm woman, Pat sounded upset and wanted to know where I was. I told her that I was sitting on the plane and we were getting ready to depart. "Get off that plane right now," she said with a note of alarm in her voice. "What?" I responded, surprised at her directness. "Get off the plane, Cheryl. It looks like there's been a terrorist attack in New York. A plane has just flown into the World Trade Center and they believe it was an intentional act." I stared at the phone. My mother-in-law is a very smart, rational woman, but at that moment, I couldn't believe what she was telling me. I thought she was overreacting. I quickly reassured her that things were okay, "It must have been a small plane, Pat, don't worry. I'll be fine." "No," she said, "you can't take that flight. This is serious. President Bush is making an announcement on television right now." That got my attention. I couldn't imagine the president addressing the nation about a small plane crash.

As I hung up the phone I promised my mother-in-law that I would stay on the ground until I knew exactly what was going on. Just then, I saw the flight attendant close the plane door. It looked like we were about to taxi out onto the runway. I stood up to alert her about my mother-in-law's message when my phone rang again. This time it was Max calling to say that she had just arrived at the airport and was heading to the gate. As it turned out, she was the last person admitted into the terminal before it was shut down for security reasons. She told me that, in fact, a large jet had crashed into the World Trade Center. She was racing to the gate as we spoke and said: "Don't let that plane take off with you on it!"

As soon as I hung up the phone with Max the pilot announced that the FAA had suspended all flights until further notice. He explained that while they were unclear about the cause, our plane would not be leaving the jetway and we would have to sit tight. I still remember feeling alarmed when a man, running to the front of the plane, demanded to be let off. The flight attendant politely, but firmly, told him that he needed to get back to his seat right away.

I couldn't even begin to take in what was happening. One minute I was heading off on a fun adventure, and the next I was surrounded by chaos and panic as people began making calls to find out what was going on. Bit by bit, the news was revealed: two jets, one American and one United, had crashed into the twin towers of the World Trade Center. Both flights had originated from our airport. There were grave concerns that additional flights had been compromised. All air traffic over the United States had been suspended indefinitely and Logan Airport was in lockdown.

Everything seemed to be moving in slow motion. My mind couldn't begin to comprehend the extent of what was happening. A few minutes later we were escorted off of the plane and told to remain in the gate area. As I stepped off the jetway I saw Max standing in a corner with a blank look on her face. We hugged and found a spot on the floor where we could sit and wait it out.

It was pure madness at this point. We were confined to the gate area while state police searched the airport for additional suspects. Cell phones were working sporadically and whenever a passenger received a call, he or she would announce the latest report. As soon as someone reported that another flight had crashed into the Pentagon I started to panic. I frantically tried to reach my husband Michael to let him know I was safe, but I couldn't get through. Then, my assistant, Jan, called crying. She was relieved to hear that my flight had not taken off and wanted me to know that my family was desperate to find me. Max and I quickly made arrangements for her to call our families and I continued trying to reach Michael. When I finally got through, I was relieved to discover that he had been asleep and unaware of what was going on. When I told him to turn on the television, he was stunned. Like all of us, he couldn't believe what he was seeing. Now Michael was scared. "Cheryl, come home!" he said. "Get out of the airport right now!"

It would be three hours before Max and I were allowed to leave the airport. As I think back to that day, I feel a bit embarrassed to admit that once Max and I arrived at my house, we watched the television reports for a short time and then went straight to the beach. We walked most of the afternoon and barely talked about what had happened. Of course, I now understand why. I couldn't face the feelings that were stirring inside. The destruction and loss of life was incomprehensible. I was also experiencing something I had never dealt with before—survivor's guilt. Deep inside I was wrestling with the fact that hundreds of people had lost their lives in an unthinkable, senseless act of violence and my life had been spared.

Three weeks after the event, the impact of 9/11 hit me full force. During a massage, my therapist placed her hand over my heart and I burst into tears. Immediately, in my mind, I saw a replay of the planes crashing into the towers over and over again. My sobs were deep, dredging up the unexpressed rage, grief, and guilt from the events of that day. Even as I recall the story here, I feel a need to tread lightly. There are still so many raw emotions and so much sadness for the families and friends who lost loved ones that morning.

As it was for people around the world, September 11 was more than a wake-up call to me; it was an emotional earthquake that sent shockwaves through my entire life. Now, in addition to questioning my career decisions, I was questioning my life: "If September 11 had been my last day on earth, would I have been content with the life I've lived thus far? What hadn't I done or accomplished that my soul really wanted to do? Was I spending enough time with my loved ones? Was I prepared for my own death?"

As I considered these questions I thought back to my experience with Lucy so long ago. I remembered what she taught me about what really matters most at the end of our lives. The tragedy of 9/11 had given me an enormous gift. In the deepest part of my soul I knew that any amount of money, fame, or best-selling books wouldn't matter one iota at the end of my life. What really mattered was my relationship with God, the people I loved, and how I was going to use this precious life I had been allowed to keep.

I also knew from experience that the best way to respond to a wake-up call was to take a good hard look at how I was living my life. Following the attacks, I turned to my journal and began answering these questions:

- What do I really want at this time in my life? Do I even know?
- What do I think I'm supposed to want?
- What are my soul priorities?
- What are my head priorities?
- How much of what I want is really for others?
- If I were to fully honor my soul priorities, what might I be afraid of losing? What might I be afraid of gaining?
- Where will I find true security now that life has become so uncertain?

As I answered these questions honestly I could see very clearly that the conflict I was experiencing reflected a power struggle between my head and soul. First, so much of what I was doing stemmed from what I thought I *should* want. For example, now that I had established a national presence, my head told me that I needed to focus on building an even larger audience. My soul, on the other hand said, "Slow down and take some time to be sure that you're headed in the right direction. Make sure that you're pursuing projects that are aligned with your values and most important needs."

I could see that I was tangled up in the game of constantly raising the bar on myself, an old pattern I learned while working in the family business. I also realized something else. At this point I had accomplished much more than I ever thought possible. It was as though my head and body were running full speed ahead working diligently to achieve the next goal, while my heart and soul were screaming, "Wait!" I needed time to catch up to myself. I was reminded of something Thomas said years ago after I made several major life changes: "When what had been your ceiling now becomes your floor, your emotional self will need time to catch up with your physical reality."

The problem was clear. When faced with important decisions, I was back to reacting by reflex, rather than making choices from a more centered, inner-directed place. Now that I had a better understanding of what was happening, I was faced with an interesting challenge.

At the time, several projects needed my attention. For example, my third book was about to be published which meant I would have to spend a lot of time on the road touring. I was also completing a pilot for my first television show, and had two national public television specials in the works. As it turned out, my pilot was picked up, and I would be asked to produce and host a five-part reality series based on my work. So, rather than pull back from the demands of my life, I made a decision to honor my commitments and walk the path of grace, trusting that all was happening exactly as it should be. The real challenge would be to apply what I was learning about surrender and patience while operating in the real world. Through all of this, the words of the great saint Paramahansa Yogananda kept running through my mind: "We must learn to be in the world and not of it."

Over the next year I traveled extensively, launched my next book, and completed my television projects. I did my best to practice good self-care while on the road, but balancing a busy life wasn't easy. There were many times when I looked at my colleagues who were writing books, hosting television shows, and traveling all the time, and wondered why I had such a hard time doing what they did. A year later, when I finally took some time off to rest and reconnect with my spiritual center, I began to understand why. While I had learned to ignite grace in my own life, it was time to enroll in a more advanced course. I needed to let my inner life and my connection to God lead the dance.

Experiment: Ignite Grace

This experiment is designed to help you learn how to ignite grace in your life. Here are the steps:

1. *Set a Goal*—Choose a goal or project for this exercise. Be specific. It could be that you want to save $1,000 in six months, clean and organize the garage, or meet a new partner. Once you have a specific goal in mind, write it down in your journal.

    Then, write down the following prayer and repeat it out loud:

    I trust in a higher purpose for my life. Please allow this or something better to occur.

2. *Adopt New Beliefs*—Ask someone who has accomplished a similar goal about his or her beliefs. Then, in your journal, write down two that inspire you most.

3. *Trust Your Gut*—Close your eyes and bring your attention inward. What actions do you need to take first? Pay
attention to how you feel both physically and emotionally, and when ideas come to mind, write them down.

4. *Get into Action*—Ask the person who accomplished a
similar goal to describe the action steps they took to
achieve it. Then, make a list of at least three steps you'll
take to get started. Remember, you must take action to
fan the flame of grace.

Now use this new version of the prayer you used earlier.
Write it in your journal and repeat it to yourself throughout
the day:

> *I am now open to receiving the gift of grace. I ask to be
> shown exactly what I need to do to achieve this goal or
> something better.*

Throughout the day, pay close attention to any signs,
messages, or inklings that may signal your next step. For
example, you may cross paths with someone who offers you
important advice or information. Or you may be invited to
attend an event that could advance your career. You might
even get a piece of mail that inspires you to try something
new. Grace is often wrapped in unexpected packages so be
willing to dig a little deeper to uncover the gift.

As you continue to work toward achieving your goal,
don't ignore your instincts or gut reactions. If you feel like
you're headed in the wrong direction, consider turning
around sooner rather than later. Use this exercise as a way
to practice surrender and patience. If you start to feel too

attached to the outcome, surrender and patiently wait for your next move to reveal itself. You may also want to hang a sign in your home and/or office that says:

Surrender and be patient. Grace is on the way.

Resources

BOOKS

The Dynamic Laws of Prosperity by Catherine Ponder (DeVorss & Company, 1985)

> *A powerful book teaching the reader about the true meaning of prosperity and how to achieve it.*

The Power of Intention by Wayne Dyer (Hay House, 2004)

> *Using an array of true stories and examples, the author teaches readers the importance of using their power and positive energy in everyday life to connect with and achieve personal abundance and success.*

Power through Constructive Thinking by Emmet Fox (Harper San Francisco, 1989)

> *Originally published in 1932, this is a timeless book of inspiring essays and practical advice on using the power of the mind to create your best life.*

The Science of Mind by Ernest Holmes (Jeremy P. Tarcher, 1997)

> *A spiritual classic which explains how to pray and meditate, offering the reader ways to master the powers of the mind in order to find purpose in life.*

MAGAZINES

Spirituality and Health

One of my favorite magazines, filled with the wisdom of a variety of spiritual traditions and great stories on the link between spirtuality and science.

WEBSITES

www.ammachi.org

This is the official website of Ammachi, the hugging saint and humanitarian who has dedicated her life to being of service to others.

6

---◆---

BALANCE SILENCE WITH ACTIVITY

If you're like most people, there are probably many days when your life feels like it's spinning out of control. You may be trying to squeeze grocery shopping and health-care appointments between work obligations and extracurricular activities. Or, you may simply feel overwhelmed by the number of choices you're forced to make every day. For example, in 2004, *Consumer Reports* offered comparisons for over 200 new cars, 200 breakfast cereals, 500 health insurance policies, and 40 household soaps! We also have access to more information than we'll ever need. Computers, which were supposed to make our lives easier, have just added more work to our already full plates. And e-mail, which has us living in fear of spam and the next fatal virus, has turned out to consume more time and attention than writing letters or licking stamps. I'm sure it's just a matter of time before there's a reality show that pits multitaskers against each other to see just how many balls they can effectively keep in the air.

I don't know about you, but I'm not very good at juggling. After a year of managing several major projects and traveling nonstop to promote my third book, I was ready to let a few balls drop so I could gain some perspective on my life. While the idea of being on television or traveling around the country may sound exciting, for me, the novelty was short-lived. Like a parent or business owner who works more than full time, I realized that while my work was rewarding, it required a great deal of effort and continually pulled me away from my spiritual center and the precious, intimate time I needed for myself and with loved ones. I wasn't sure I wanted to make that kind of sacrifice.

After working so hard, it was difficult for me to slow down. My body was so used to running on adrenaline that when faced with an open schedule, I found myself searching for ways to fill it. I had to keep reminding myself of a message I used to give clients—beyond boredom is serenity. Regaining a sense of balance required me to be disciplined. So I started by creating a routine. I got up early each morning and spent time meditating and recording my dreams. Then, when I felt tempted to fill the void by looking for things to do, I focused on my commitment to relax and simply be. I knew that if I surrendered my need to make things happen and allowed grace to lead, the next stage of my life would find me.

———◆———

In May of 2002, my friend Max called to tell me she had signed up for a silent retreat. I consider Max to be my spiritual sister, a soulmate who is equally committed to walking a conscious path. We've been friends for more than thirteen years, and she's been by my side through the ups and downs of my career. Max knew that I was rethinking my direction in life and that my spiritual well-being had become a central theme. When she mentioned that she was attending a retreat about mystical spirituality and achieving a direct experience of God, I was anxious to find out more.

The leader of the retreat was Jerry Thomas, a former scientist who shifted gears and began practicing a monastic way of life. His study of quantum physics led him to surmise that there was an underlying intelligence supporting all of creation. His desire to understand this intelligence prompted his search for a source.

Jerry's exploration began with an in-depth study of historical, sacred scriptures from mystical Judaism (kabbalah), Christianity, Sufism, Hinduism, and Buddhism. During his investigation, he identified a common thread that unified all the traditions: the deep experience of silence and the presence of the Divine within. It turned out that what he was searching for was the core subject matter of the teachings of mystics and saints of all religions and traditions.

Jerry's quest for knowledge and understanding led him to join a monastery where he would live in silence for several years. Then, after leaving the monastery, he traveled to India, the Middle East, and throughout Europe to study the teachings of those who had attained God-Realization, the ultimate manifestation of a mystical way of life. At this point Jerry came to recognize the intelligence for what it truly was—grace. In fact, it was the subject of grace and his experience of Divine Unity (known throughout the ages as mystical spirituality) that captured his mind and heart.

When Max heard about Jerry's background and the fact that he was an expert in the mystical teachings of the five major traditions, she decided to attend one of his retreats. By the end of the weekend, she was so moved by her experience that she called and left me a message the moment she got into her car. Little did I know that her words would inspire the next phase of my spiritual adventure. "Cheryl, this is exactly where you need to be," she said, "the answer you're looking for is in the silence."

By now I was keenly aware that people are often ambassadors of grace, so I paid close attention to Max's message. Her wisdom had served me well in the past. Whenever I felt confused or at a crossroad in my life, she seemed to know exactly what to say to return me to my spiritual center. In this case, her excitement about the retreat encouraged me to check it out for myself.

TAKING A RETREAT FROM LIFE

If I could offer you only one gift, it would be an opportunity to retreat from your busy life long enough to experience the insight that comes from having a reserve of emotional and physical space. Too often the choice is made for us when we get sick, or face some kind of life crisis that gives us a reprieve from our everyday tasks and responsibilities. Typically when this happens, though, we're focused on how bad we feel or what we need to do to handle the problem. Fortunately my client Kimberly didn't let this happen. When she was forced to leave work to address a serious health concern, she saw it as an opportunity to take a good, hard look at the state of her life. Consequently, she took radical action to make things better for herself and her family.

Kimberly was diagnosed with a benign tumor in her uterus that caused severe blood loss during her menstrual cycle. When it reached the point that her illness interfered with her ability to work and care for her children, Kimberly was forced to acknowledge how serious the situation truly was. Married, with two children, she worked full time for a biotech company and had very little time for herself. During one of our first conversations she admitted, "I've given my life to my job. It takes so much out of me that I have very little energy left for my husband and children. As a result, I'm always exhausted and rarely happy."

Whenever I work with a client, I pay very close attention to his or her language—their specific choice of words. When I thought about what was happening with Kimberly's body, it was apparent that her statement, "It takes so much out of me," was in a very real sense reflecting the fact that she was losing life energy, in this case, her blood. Kimberly's health was literally draining out of her body.

Once it was evident that her condition was serious, I suggested to Kimberly that she try to negotiate a new arrangement with her boss. After several conversations with her husband and a meeting with a financial planner, it was decided that Kimberly would ask her boss if it was possible to work part time. Both Kimberly and her husband agreed that if her request was denied, she would almost certainly have to leave.

Although it's unusual for a company to renegotiate the terms of an executive position, Kimberly's boss recognized how important she was to the organization. He agreed to let her work part time for one year. During our next conversation, when she shared the good news, Kimberly said she felt both elated and terrified. Having worked so hard for so long, she was afraid to slow down and confront the truth about herself and her life—that her fear of financial hardship was fueling her work addiction, and as it turned out, her illness. In this type of situation it's not uncommon to have conflicting feelings. It's as though our head screams, "Fear!" while our soul jumps for joy. Kimberly's decision to turn inward was a critically important step. The result, as you'll see a little later, turned out to be much more than she bargained for.

FINDING GRACE IN THE SILENCE

In September of 2002 I had a new introduction to a deeper part of myself by attending my first retreat. It was called "Inner Silence." It only took one evening for me to know that Max was absolutely right. It was exactly what I needed. The retreat consisted of short lectures about the mystical teachings of the five major traditions combined with periods of chanting and deep meditation. There were only thirty-five attendees and the accommodations were modest and simple—the perfect environment for inner reflection.

When I arrived, I unpacked my things, made myself a cup of tea, and headed for the meeting hall to find a comfortable chair. The theme of this particular retreat was what Jerry called "reaching the pure state of the Soul," a quiet, inner state of silence that can heal the mind, rest the body, and enliven one's state of consciousness. His teaching was based on a contemplative perspective of religion through which one could achieve a more direct and complete experience of God. I appreciated that Jerry's intention was to help participants *experience* a feeling of oneness with the Divine, as opposed to getting caught up in a particular doctrine or religious dogma. I couldn't wait to get started.

The retreat opened with a lecture. Jerry asked us to put away our pens and notebooks. He wanted us to disengage the analytical part of our minds so we could relax and let the material seep into our consciousness. Several of us panicked at the thought of not being able to take notes. We were afraid that we would miss or forget something important. But Jerry quickly explained that the retreat wasn't about acquiring information, it was about having an experience. "Mystical spirituality is primarily about one's relationship with God," he said. "The goal of this retreat is to help strengthen your connection to the God within. Once you experience this connection, you'll be able to access it more easily in your everyday life."

Jerry's teaching style was refreshing. He was very wise, had a terrific sense of humor, and didn't take himself too seriously. Having studied both science and silence, Jerry had a compelling way of combining the subtle concepts of spirituality with concrete practical application. And it was the alignment of spirituality with practicality that I, once again, found most appealing.

I was impressed by Jerry's ability to weave science and spirituality together during his lectures. For example, he talked at length about how the writings of great saints and scriptures were infused with the consciousness of the writer. Jerry believed that sacred texts like the Bible or the Bhagavad-Gita (as important to Hindus as the Bible is here in the West) had the ability to affect a reader's consciousness in a powerful way. To lend credence to his statement, he

described an informal study he conducted with several colleagues at a major university.

The study was designed to test a person's galvanic skin
response and brain wave function before and after reading
three types of documents. The first paper was written by a
person who was mentally ill. The second was an uplifting
story written by a social psychologist. The third combined
the teachings of three different saints: Paramahansa
Yogananda, Rumi, and St. Therese Lisieux.

The results were intriguing. When the study group read
the writing from the person who was mentally ill, the physiologic response was agitation. The readers felt unsettled and
out of balance. When they read the story from the psychologist, their response showed an increased level of calmness.
However, when the group read the passages written by three
saints they went into a deep state of relaxation and reported
subjectively, a sense of enhanced inner well-being. Although
the results were speculative, Jerry felt confident that the
study clearly demonstrated how people *attune* themselves to
the consciousness of the writer. Based on his knowledge of
physics, Jerry held a firm belief that because everything is
connected, it was only natural to assume that when we bring
someone or something into our awareness, we begin to res-
onate with it. "The mind is like water," he said, "it will take
the form of the container you pour it into." Being a skeptic
at heart and someone with a highly inquisitive mind, it was
helpful for me to hear Jerry's scientific perspective. It gave
my new spiritual studies more validity and substance.

When the time came for meditation, Jerry reminded us
that the nature of the mind was to think. But rather than
telling us to empty our minds and stop thinking, he encour-

aged us to work *with* our minds by repeating sacred sounds or a mantra. "By using a mantra," he said, "one can gently coax the mind into a restful state and then slip into the silence 'between the notes.'" Then, teaching us an Eastern prayer, Jerry asked us to repeat it to ourselves as we started to meditate. Instantly I was reminded of praying the rosary as a young girl. I always loved the feeling of stillness and calm I would get from repeating prayers. In fact, I felt so comforted by this that I continue to use repetitive prayer to calm myself when I feel agitated, anxious, or stressed.

One of the things I appreciated most about the retreat was that Jerry called upon the wisdom of all of the major traditions rather than focusing on one in particular. Because I was raised in the Catholic Church with the Bible as my only source of spiritual information, I was pleased to learn that every major religion had, at its core, the same fundamental message: "Our basic nature is Divine, while our human experience is transient or temporal." A recognition that we are all children of God and that we have an innate desire to merge with this Divine Oneness was at the center of all the major traditions.

The weekend was also filled with long periods of chanting and meditation. Although I had meditated off and on over the years, I would usually practice for short periods of time. Now we were being asked to sit for forty-five minutes. As we began to do so, Jerry reminded us to keep it simple. "Don't *try* to meditate," he said. "Just allow yourself to be with the silence. Trying to control your mind is like fighting with a pig. When you fight with a pig two things will happen. Number one, you get dirty. And, number two, the pig likes it. The mind is always searching for happiness and attempting to find it in an unbalanced way. It looks outside for happiness because it's never been shown how to see that the source of all happiness is within. Once it gets a taste of *this* happiness, it will naturally want to go back for more. So, rather than struggle, we'll do something the mind likes— we'll use the mantra to enchant the mind into a deeper state of bliss."

For the first twenty or thirty minutes of my meditation, I had trouble relaxing my mind. "I'm no good at meditating," I thought. "I'm too unfocused and tense and I'll never be able to calm myself down." This kind of internal struggle and self-doubt was a reflection of my everyday life. I was always battling with myself about something. And rarely did I feel like a winner.

Each time I recognized that I had gotten off track, I returned my attention to the mantra. As we approached the end of the first meditation period, I finally experienced what I now see as a "moment of grace." I lost track of time and had no sense of my physical body. My consciousness had gently slipped into the space between my thoughts. As I had heard others describe, I felt an overwhelming sense of being at one with all living things and I started to weep. In my brief moment of bliss it felt like I had merged with love itself. I came out of the meditation feeling joyful and rested. It only took this brief encounter with the deep peace of silence to know that I wanted more.

◆

Kimberly came to discover the peace of silence in a totally different way. As part of her healing process, Kimberly spent time researching alternative methods for healing the tumor in her uterus. She found the book *Women's Bodies, Women's Wisdom* by Dr. Christiane Northrup to be particularly helpful. In it, Dr. Northrup recommended the use of a castor oil pack on the abdomen for one hour a day. The idea was to use the castor oil compress to soothe and heal the uterus while quietly meditating and listening for any messages she might receive from her body.

Kimberly admitted that at first, her motivation for doing this was her hope that the castor oil pack would somehow cause the tumor to disappear. She started by spending fifteen or twenty minutes quietly listening to her body. Over time, though, she spent more time meditating. She began to look forward to the comforting warmth of the pack on her abdomen and the peace she felt as she learned to lose herself in this quiet time. Silence is good self-care. When we calm the mind, we flood the body with health-enhancing chemicals and gain access to important information about who we are, how we feel, and what we need.

Over the next year, Kimberly began several new activities that helped her feel more centered and self-aware. In addition to a regular meditation practice, she joined a therapist-led woman's group designed to help its members take a more conscious role in creating and directing their lives. She also spent more time with her children, and was reminded of the amazing lessons that children can teach us about living in the moment, the importance of fun, and enjoying simple pleasures. Kimberly admitted, "I had been so busy with work that I completely lost touch with the gifts that my children have to offer. Looking back, I can see that I operated on autopilot, trudging through my daily life like a robot, efficiently handling my professional responsibilities while waiting patiently for the opportunity, and permission, to start enjoying my life. When I think about this it makes me feel so sad. It was such a waste of time."

At the end of the year Kimberly decided that she would not return to work full time. Instead, she left the company and did something she'd thought about since her early days in college. She took a job teaching high school in her hometown. "As a child, I had so much admiration for my teachers. They introduced me to new worlds and inspired my curiosity for life. Now I'm doing the same thing for other children. I love the idea of helping to shape their minds, while at the same time being able to spend more time with my family. Even though as a teacher I'm making less money, the quality of my life, as well as the quality of my family's life, has become a more important priority—one that brings us far more value than the income I used to earn."

———◆———

My first silent retreat was a very special experience. Max was right. The answers I was searching for were in the silence. In the past, meditation meant quieting my mind long enough to hear my intuition or inner wisdom. Now I was beginning to understand something more important— *the answer was the silence itself.*

I left my first retreat knowing that I needed to make meditation a bigger and more consistent part of my life. I felt so nourished by my experience that I made a commitment to attend more silent retreats over the next year. I wanted to immerse myself in the study of mystical spirituality and most important, I wanted to get back to the place of deep peace I had found during my meditation.

Over the next several months I began to enjoy spending time away from the world as I used to know it. I was learning a lot from my meditation experiences, the retreat lectures from Jerry, and my fellow participants. And as this new phase of my life unfolded I became even more aware of how grace was influencing my life. For example, one weekend I noticed that several people were using prayer beads while meditating. I immediately thought of a special set of rosary beads I carried around in my purse. They had been an unexpected gift I received earlier in the year in a most unusual way.

One night, during dinner with my friend Chris, we had a conversation about the spiritual practices we used in our everyday life. Chris mentioned that she loved to pray the rosary before going to bed and that it had become an important ritual that prepared her for sleep. I explained that I too had prayed the rosary as a young girl, but had forgotten how to do it. She offered to send me instructions. One week later I received a prayer card from Chris in the mail and I put it by my bed to remind me to purchase a set of rosary beads.

About a month went by and I had completely forgotten about the beads. Then, one morning on my way to the post office, I pulled up to the front of the building, gathered my things and opened the car door. When my foot touched the pavement, I noticed that I had parked directly over a drainage grate. Just then, something shiny caught my eye. I took a closer look and discovered a beautiful set of black rosary beads hanging on the edge of the grate. I quickly reached down to scoop them up and checked with the post office to see if anyone had asked about them. But no one had. As I left my name and number with the clerk behind the counter, I knew in my heart that this gift was for me. I remember thinking, "This is no coincidence. I'm sure these beads are a symbol of what's to come." I said a silent prayer of thanks and headed home. Now, here I was, several months later, pulling them out of my bag to use while meditating at the retreat.

THE LINK BETWEEN SCIENCE AND SILENCE

As neuroscientists develop new technology to observe brain wave patterns and physiologic changes during periods of deep silence, the benefits of meditation are becoming more apparent. While in the process of researching this, a friend introduced me to the work of Bill Harris, founder of Centerpointe Research Institute. Bill has written extensively on what happens to the brain during meditation. He has even created audio technology that helps people achieve deep states of relaxation while improving their ability to handle stress. I found Bill's work so fascinating that I called him to talk about it. During our conversation and my subsequent inquiries, I learned a lot about the brain and how it's affected by meditation.

The brain operates in four patterns:

Beta—As the most active brain wave pattern, beta is the primary state that most of us operate in throughout the day. This is the general pattern of normal waking consciousness, and when our brains produce high levels of beta waves we tend to feel anxious and restless.

Alpha—The second brain wave pattern, alpha, is the state associated with a deeper, more relaxed state of mind. This is the brain wave pattern that most meditators experience.

It's also the in-between state we experience just before falling asleep.

Theta—Theta is the brain wave pattern of dreaming sleep. This pattern is associated with higher levels of creativity, improved memory function, and increased ability to learn new skills. Long-term, experienced meditators are capable of entering this state while remaining aware of their surroundings.

Delta—Finally, Delta is the slowest brain wave pattern of all, a deeply relaxed state usually associated with dreamless sleep.

At any moment, all four of these patterns are present to varying degrees. For example, while you're communicating or analyzing information, your brain is making lots of beta waves. At the same time it's making delta waves that regulate body functions. When we meditate, we increase the amount of slower brain wave patterns, particularly alpha waves, and in doing so, we gradually enter into deeper states of relaxation. So, if you've had a busy day and you're feeling stressed, there's a good chance that your brain wave function is being dominated by beta patterns and you're operating in what's called a high beta state. When you begin to meditate, it's not uncommon to have difficulty transitioning from this state. As a result, you may feel irritable or unsettled at first. Fortunately, using a mantra, repeating a prayer, or focusing on your breath, will automatically slow down your brain waves. As a matter of fact, simply closing your eyes will result in increased alpha (relaxed) brain wave patterns. The good news is that the more you practice, the easier it will be for you to enter into a deeper state (or a slower brain wave cycle).

While meditation allows us to slow our brain waves so we're able to enter a peaceful state, it also results in something called brain synchrony, a rebalancing of the two hemispheres of the brain. This phenomenon was discovered in the 1970s using EEG studies on experienced meditators. The subjects of this study not only slowed their brain waves and entered into a deep state of relaxation; they also experienced something called whole-brain integration. This is important to note because people usually use one side of their brain much more than the other.

When your life gets hectic and you feel out of balance, there's a good chance that two things are happening. First, your brain is making lots of beta wave patterns, causing you to feel a heightened sense of awareness and/or agitation. Second, one hemisphere of your brain is probably working harder than the other, creating an imbalance in brain function. So, when you feel out of sorts, it may be because your brain is literally out of balance—the left and right hemispheres of your brain may not be in synch.

In many respects, an out of balance life may be fueled by an out of balance brain. When this is the case, trying to get more organized or to manage your time more efficiently can actually exacerbate the problem. Meditating, which alters your brain waves, addresses the problem at its source. Viewed from this perspective, the practice of meditation may be the best time management tool there is.

It's interesting to note that when we feel the most overwhelmed, we often attempt to think our way through a problem or work harder to get things done. If we could learn to stop, close our eyes, and pay attention to our breath or repeat a mantra or prayer long enough to restore some balance to our brain, we would find ourselves in a more relaxed and resourceful state of mind—one where we'd make smarter and less impulsive decisions.

Perhaps you've already had this experience without realizing it. For example, you get stumped by a problem at work and decide to take a break. You close your eyes to rest for a while and some time later the solution pops into your head. Or, perhaps you've had a disagreement with a family member that leaves you feeling angry and resentful. But then, after a short nap, you're suddenly able to see his or her point of view. I've come to see that resting and rebalancing the brain is often the most effective and efficient problem-solving tool there is.

We've already established that meditation helps us relax and create a balanced state of mind. Research has also shown that meditation makes the brain more resilient, raising the threshold of what we can handle. It's as if your brain capacity is expanded, allowing you to withstand and process higher levels of stress. One of the reasons this happens is because the practice of meditation allows the meditator to develop a witnessing perspective—the ability to watch how he or she responds to a given situation. Once you're able to see the link between your thoughts, actions, and emotional states, you can be more conscious about *how you allow yourself to think*. So, if you find yourself ruminating over a problem at home, or stewing about the stalled traffic when you're late for an appointment, you'll be better able to recognize this unresourceful pattern of thinking and interrupt it. Eventually, this will allow your brain to handle higher levels of stress without going on tilt.

There is also an interesting link between science and spirituality with regard to brain function. Experienced meditators report that as their state of relaxation deepens they begin to feel a sense of interconnectedness with all things. The lines between us and them, or you and me start to blur and are replaced with a visceral sense that we're all connected and that our individual actions affect everything around us. We also bring our consciousness into present moment time. Without worrying about the past or future, we experience a profound sense of peace and confidence that all is happening as it should. The more we meditate, the less affected we are by external events, and the more comforted we feel in general. Science confirms this. When our brain wave patterns slow down and the hemispheres of the brain become balanced, test subjects report feeling a sense of oneness and inner peace.

Bill Harris has used the results of his research to develop state-of-the-art audio technology that assists people in achieving deep states of meditation (see the resource section at the end of this chapter for more information). This tool, called Holosync, uses a refinement of something called binaural beat technology—very precise combinations of sine wave audio tones—to stimulate the deeper brain wave patterns that result from meditation. I've used it extensively as an adjunct to my normal practice and have experienced impressive results. Not only does Holosync allow the listener to enter deep states of relaxation more effectively, it balances both hemispheres, makes the brain more resilient, and causes us to feel less vulnerable to the effects of stress.

THE MYTH OF SUCCESS

Not only was I experiencing the beneficial effects of meditation, my study of mystical spirituality and the practice of silence was providing me with insights that changed my worldview. One of my most profound lessons reflected what saints and scientists had been saying for centuries. We live in a world of duality where there is light and dark, good and bad, health and sickness, pleasure and pain. This universal law is in direct contrast to our pursuit for everlasting happiness. According to the law of duality, any period of success, prosperity, or joy will be followed at some point or another by a period of failure, loss, or disappointment. It's a scientific law. This is often most noticeable when we're too focused on achieving material things, believing that they'll bring us long-lasting peace of mind and fulfillment. Holding onto this idea is like putting your money in a bad investment. Eventually you lose. Think about it. Do you know anyone who's been able to create long-lasting happiness by focusing solely on what they can accomplish or accumulate?

Understanding this law helped me to realize why I often worried about when the next shoe might drop, even when things were going well. I used to think it was related to a fear of success or scarcity thinking. But, I was missing the bigger picture. At some point or another, the other shoe *will* drop. You will lose a client, a loved one will pass on, or your luck will run out. This is why it's so important to invest more energy in developing your inner assets—your spiritual life. This means building a strong relationship with a Higher Power, finding the courage to surrender your will, and maintaining a commitment to balance activity with silence. These investments will not only bring you greater value, but also give you the strength to weather any storm; ultimately, they will give you the peace and happiness you long for. The more you enter the silence, the less you will be ruled by the physical world.

I remember discussing this idea with an audience member during one of my presentations. She was an exuberant red-haired woman with a bright smile and a cheerful disposition. She explained that she had started a consulting business a year earlier and things were going extremely well. "I've experienced amazing growth in my business this year," she said. "I have a large client base and I'm excited about the future. It's just that every now and then there's a little voice in my head that says, 'Watch out, at any time, it could all come crumbling down.'"

My first response was heartfelt, yet direct. "It *could* come crumbling down," I said, "and that's the point. Your little voice is delivering an important message from your soul. It's telling you to invest as much time in your spiritual self as you are in your business. If you put all your success eggs into your company's basket, you put your emotional and spiritual well-being at risk. At some point you may, in fact, lose some clients, or you might become ill and need to take time off. But by strengthening and developing your spiritual core, you'll remain steady and rooted to your soul. You'll be able to handle any situation that comes your way. So here's the lesson: From now on, each time you hear that little voice, consider it a reminder to do something that connects you to your spiritual center and a power greater than yourself. That's not only the key to success in business, it's the key to success in life."

FINDING TRUTH IN THE SILENCE

When I decided to slow down and take time off to rest, I honestly considered walking away from all I had created. Now, rather than give up my work or indulge in my fantasy of moving to a mountainside monastery, the real trick would be to maintain a sense of inner peace while living and participating in the world. This was the gift that silence would bring—the understanding that the quality of my outer life would always depend on the quality of my inner life, not on the status of my career, checkbook, or relationship. Too many people still believe that they are their bank accounts, their business cards, or their addresses. But this belief just feeds the illusion that our power exists in the physical world. The truth is that we are spiritual beings. Our souls transcend time and space, and our true power resides within. If you want your outer world to be peaceful, calm, and filled with joy, you don't need to acquire more time or take a vacation from life, you need to cultivate this inner state of being.

I also realized that the more I practiced silence, the more effective I would be in the world. Because if we are, in fact, affected by the consciousness of the writers and teachers we study, my commitment to raise my own consciousness would be the greatest gift I could ever give to anyone. So with the end of each retreat, nurturing my spiritual life became a greater priority. At first I preferred the lectures to the periods of meditation. But, over time, my soul longed for the silence.

ENTERING THE STATE OF GRACE

If you're like most people, the idea of quieting your mind may feel like an impossible feat, especially with all the stimulation that exists in the world today. But I can assure you that you can do it, if you're patient and willing to take it one small step at a time. Most people give up too soon because they can't sit still or they can't stop thinking about everything they have to do. But, it's important to know that it's normal to feel restless, agitated, or bored when you first begin to meditate. It's like trying to cool down an engine that's been revving too high, for too long.

As you start to meditate, it's important to hang on through the period of restlessness even if you only get a glimpse of the peaceful feeling you can expect over time. And, remove any preconceived notions of what it means to meditate in the right way. Everyone's experience is different. While there are things you can do to help you relax, like using a mantra or paying attention to your breath, trust your own instincts and experience. As you practice, you'll find your own way to the joy that exists in the silence.

For me, the process of meditating is like entering a house with the intention of making my way to a quiet room at the center of the building. As I pass through the first few rooms I may hear some noise, but as I move further inward, through doors that lead to smaller rooms, the noise level gradually decreases. Once I reach my destination, there is nothing but silence. The more I meditate the more familiar this process becomes. At first I sit and breathe normally. Then I usually start to think about tasks I need to complete, things that happened during the day, or situations that feel unsettling. In fact, it's quite common to focus on painful or uncomfortable experiences. Your mind is programmed to think, and when it's overstimulated, it looks for something to focus on in an effort to organize itself. Usually, what comes up first is something you're worried about, like the argument you had with your spouse, overdue bills, or the sarcastic comment you heard from a friend.

As my mind shifts from one thought to another, I simply breathe and repeat a mantra (or prayer) to ease myself into a calmer state. Then, as I start to relax, I can feel myself being slowly pulled inward, away from the external world. Regardless of how often I meditate, each experience is different. Sometimes I'm able to reach a relaxed state within minutes, other times not at all. My only goal is to go wherever the meditation takes me, and to keep at it, regardless of what happens.

Remember that any period of stillness, regardless of the quality, is nourishing to your body, mind, and spirit. As a matter of fact, once you enter a deeply relaxed state, don't be surprised if you fall asleep, especially if you're sleep deprived, which unfortunately, is more the rule than the exception these days. In the past, before I knew much about meditation, I would discount the experience when I fell asleep, telling myself that it didn't count. Now I know better. Even if you fall asleep, you'll still get something from the experience. When your brain waves slow down, your mind becomes more balanced and integrated, and this will help you feel rested, calm, and refreshed when you wake.

Going into the silence is like taking a bath in pure, white light—it clears you, calms you, and quiets you; and it helps you manage the stress of normal everyday life. It's in the silence that we have our greatest opportunity to access the power of grace.

As much as I know that most of you would love a three-step plan, unfortunately it's not that simple. As you try the experiment at the end of this chapter, remember that committing to meditate will require you to make space in your busy life. But think of the amazing benefits—less suffering, less fear, and a clearer sense of yourself as a soul—a Divine Being who exists beyond physical death.

FIND YOUR SPIRITUAL SANITY

Granted, it's hard to find time for silence when you have children, responsibilities, and commitments at work. However, your spiritual sanity depends on it. When working on the experiment at the end of this chapter, keep the following guidelines in mind:

- *Meditate for life.* Rather than meditate for some kind of mystical or *aha* experience, meditate for life. The goal is to bring your brain, heart, and soul into balance so you can access the deep well of peace that exists within you. The more you meditate, the easier it will be to see and access the grace that already exists in your life. Don't make your spiritual life a goal-directed plan. The only objective is to show up and practice so you can deepen your experience.

- *Embrace your imperfection.* There is no right way to meditate. The way in which you enter the silence will change over time. When you find yourself trying too hard, or berating yourself for not keeping your commitment, try this simple practice: Just sit still for five minutes. Of course, there will be days when you won't feel like meditating. Allow yourself to be where you are. Don't throw in the towel because you didn't keep your commitment. Simply return to your practice.

- *Choose something and stick with it.* Rather than using a variety of meditation techniques or tools, choose the one that feels most right to you and master it. For example, choose one prayer or mantra and use it for three months. Pay attention to what happens. In this day and age, with our lives getting busier and more complex everyday, it can be a relief to settle into a simple routine. And, as the following story demonstrates, when it comes to a spiritual practice, less is often more.

  There is a story from the lore of Sheik Nasrudin, a character from the Sufi tradition. Sheik Nasrudin had a farm in the middle of the desert. Tired of traveling a long distance to get water every day, he asked God to provide him with a source close to home. When God heard his request, he sent an angel to Nasrudin who said, "God would like you to dig a well. If you do, you'll have all the water you'll ever need." Then the angel left. Forty years later, when the angel came to bring Sheik Nasrudin to heaven, she asked him about his well. "God deceived me," Nasrudin exclaimed. "I dug one hundred wells each fifty feet deep and I never found water." With that the angel replied, "If you had dug *one* well one hundred feet deep instead of a hundred wells fifty feet deep, you would have found all the water you ever needed." Don't waste your time searching for the perfect technique. Simply choose one and go deep.

- *Create a ritual.* Choose a time of day that is favorable to your schedule. Consider this time sacred. Your mind and body crave routine. When you meditate at the same time every day, you condition yourself to relax at your appointed time.

- *Allow discipline to give you freedom.* Even though you may think that practicing silence every day will require great discipline, it's important to bear this in mind: discipline is the path to emotional and spiritual freedom. This is freedom from suffering, from feeling so attached to and seduced by the external world, and from disappointment when things don't go the way you want. As you make the practice of silence a priority, you'll discover that, instead of making you feel tense or anxious, discipline is what sets you up to feel calm and at peace.

- *Let a chant meditate* you. On days when you can't find time to meditate you can do the next best thing—listen to a chant. Remember that a chant is a sacred sound and when you listen to one you infuse yourself with the consciousness of the words. In this way it becomes a powerful way to keep yourself connected to your spiritual center, especially when you're in the middle of a crisis or feeling overwhelmed. Whether you listen to a chant, or silently chant to yourself, chanting calms and soothes you at your spiritual core. And remember, it also influences your brain wave patterns, increasing the resiliency of your brain and your ability to effectively handle stress.

These guidelines and suggestions are contrary to the messages we receive from the world around us. Instead, we're rewarded for our ability to multitask, and to be productive, fast, and efficient. This is exactly why so many people feel spiritually restless. Our souls long for our attention and acknowledgment. As you learn to balance silence with activity, you'll develop new skills to create peace and calm anywhere—on the subway, in the middle of the day at work, or even when your kids are screaming in the next room! The more you make silence a priority, the sooner you'll be released from the fear and anxiety that comes from living in an uncertain, ever-changing world. Over time you'll come to realize that the peace and joy you seek can only be found within—in that very special place in your heart that speaks the voice of your soul. When you visit this place often, grace never leaves your side.

————◆————

Experiment: Create Your Own Spiritual Practice

1. Create a private sanctuary in your home.
2. Condition your mind and body to meditate.
3. Use a chant, mantra, or prayer.
4. Wrap yourself in the consciousness of grace.

1. CREATE A PRIVATE SANCTUARY IN YOUR HOME
To enhance your meditation experience, create a private sanctuary in your home. You don't need to have a special room or large area (unless, of course, you're lucky enough to have one), just some space you can call your own. You might even create an altar where you can put sacred pictures, statues, prayer beads, or candles. Be sure to include

items you treasured from your early religious experiences, as well as those from the present.

My friend Joanne feels a strong connection to Native American spirituality. On her altar she placed special feathers she collected in her travels, pictures of Native American spiritual leaders, and an American Indian basket that contains a parcel of dried sage called a smudge stick. My friend Philip is a Buddhist. His meditation area includes a cushion, a special robe, a statue of the Buddha, a picture of his teacher, and a singing bowl.

One of the most beautiful stories I've ever heard about creating a sanctuary came from a woman I met in a workshop. Angela was a mother of three young girls. She and her husband created a very special place in their home where the family could go, together, or individually, to relax and pray. They invited their children to contribute their own spiritual symbols or objects to this place. The symbols that each of her daughters chose were beautiful and unique to their personalities. For example, her youngest (who was four years old) chose to contribute a colorful leaf from their backyard. Their middle child drew a picture of God, and the oldest found a photo of the sun streaming through a group of trees in their backyard. Angela and her husband made their own contributions to this area of their home as well.

2. CONDITION YOUR MIND AND BODY TO MEDITATE

For years, religious institutions have used rituals to create a spiritual mood. The use of incense, hymns, repetitious movement (standing, sitting, kneeling, etc.), and prayer activate sensory memories that support worship and Divine union. You can use this same idea to enhance your meditation experience. For example, you might light incense or a candle, wrap yourself in a silk shawl, listen to music, or start and end your practice with a specific prayer.

I often use this beautiful prayer by Paramahansa Yogananda:

> *Heavenly Father, Divine Mother, Friend, Beloved God, may thy love shine forever on the sanctuary of my devotion and may I be able to awaken thy love in all hearts.*

I've had clients who start their meditation practice by writing in their journals. This helps them clear their minds of anything that might prevent them from slipping into the silence. Joanne, who loves Native American spirituality, begins her practice by lighting a smudge stick and filling her room with the smell of sage. Then, she repeats a chant before being still. Philip puts on his special robe, strikes his Tibetan singing bowl to mark the beginning of his meditation practice, and recites a round of prayers on his mala (prayer beads). He then completes his practice by striking the singing bowl again.

As you design your own traditions, be sure to personalize them based on your unique spiritual beliefs. Allow your rituals to move you into a quiet place of self-reflection that inspires Divine union and peace.

3. USE A CHANT, MANTRA, OR PRAYER

Choose a sacred word, phrase, or prayer. Then, while sitting comfortably with your eyes closed, quietly repeat the mantra to yourself. Each time you become aware of intrusive thoughts, gently return your focus to your mantra. Here are some examples you might try:

- Om Sai (This Sanskrit chant embodies the consciousness of the Divine Mother and Divine Father within.)
- Lord Jesus Christ, have mercy on me. (This is a Christian prayer, commonly known as the Jesus prayer. It is said that this prayer draws grace toward us.)
- God, grant me the serenity to accept the things I cannot change, the courage to change the things I can, and the wisdom to know the difference. (A great prayer for learning to surrender.)
- All-ah (This Sufi mantra embodies the consciousness of the Divine.)
- Shalom (A Jewish mantra that embodies the consciousness of peace.)
- Om Mani Padme Hung (A Buddhist mantra of great compassion.)
- May I feel peace, May I feel peace, May I feel peace.

Not only have I used these mantras when meditating, I've also used them throughout the day. They help settle my mind and keep me centered. Having studied the efficacy of prayer, and having read extensively about the effect of sacred sounds on the mind and the body, I imagine that using a chant is like taking a daily dose of a potent spiritual vitamin. It works particularly well during times when I feel impatient. For example, I often repeat a chant while standing in line at the grocery store. (A great way to handle long lines!) In fact, I recall one instance when I imagined what a trip to the grocery store might be like if *everyone* were silently praying while standing in line. Imagine how the mood would change!

4. WRAP YOURSELF IN THE CONSCIOUSNESS OF GRACE

Keeping in mind the study Jerry referred to about how we are affected by the consciousness of others, one powerful way of keeping your spiritual practice alive is to expose yourself to the teachings of saints and spiritual masters. I try to read something of a spiritual nature every day, for example, a passage from a sacred text or book. I also watch lectures from spiritual teachers (like the monks from the Self-Realization Fellowship), or documentaries of great saints, like "The Life of Padre Pio," a Catholic priest from a small village in Italy who was blessed with the stigmata. Remember, when you read a book by a great master or spiritual teacher, you are absorbing the energy and consciousness of his or her wisdom.

Resources

BOOKS

Body of Time, Soul of Eternity by Jerry Thomas (Dawn Dancer Press, 2003)

> *This book condenses thousands of years of teachings by God-Realized Masters including Jesus, Krishna, Buddha, and Paramahansa Yogananda. The writing is clear, concise, and inspiring.*

God Talks with Arjuna: The Bhagavad Gita translated by Paramahansa Yogananda (Self-Realization Fellowship, 1995)

> *Yogananda was the great saint who brought yoga to America in the early nineteen hundreds. This holy Eastern*

text describes in both scientific and spiritual terms a clear and practical program for what Yogananda called self-realization—the awakening of oneself to his or her true Divine Self.

The Heart of the Mystic: Contemplations of Mystical Spirituality by Jerry Thomas (Dawn Dancer Press, 2003)
This book is a beautiful collection of sayings and summations of many of the great God-Realized Teachers from all spiritual traditions.

The Holy Science by Swami Sri Yukteswar (Self-Realization Fellowship, 1990)
This small book explores parallel passages from the Bible and the Hindu scriptures to reveal the essential unity of all religions.

Instinct for Freedom: Finding Liberation Through Living by Alan Clements (New World Library, 2002)
Alan was the first American to become a Buddhist monk in Burma. This book tells the story of his spiritual journey.

Meditation as Medicine: Activate the Power of Your Natural Healing by Dharma Singh Khalsa, M.D., and Cameron Stauth (Atria Books, 2002)
Proponents of the power of using your mind, body, and spirit to overcome illness, this book is an adaptation of kundalini yoga combined with meditation, using specific breathing patterns, posture and movements, mantras, and mental focus.

The Power of Now: A Guide to Spiritual Enlightenment by Eckardt Tolle (New World Library, 1999)
This book offers practical strategies for living in present moment time.

Sermon on the Mount According to Vedanta by Swami Prabhavananda (Vedanta Press, 1991)

> *This book is a Hindu perspective on the teachings of Jesus Christ according to Vedanta, an Eastern tradition that believes our real nature is Divine and the goal of existence is to unfold and express that Divinity.*

Sermon on the Mount: The Key to Success in Life by Emmet Fox (Harper San Francisco, 1989)

> *In this book Fox shares his interpretation of the metaphysical teachings of Jesus Christ.*

Thresholds of the Mind by Bill Harris (Centerpointe Press, 2002)

> *This book contains fascinating information and research on the workings of the human mind as well as scientific evidence of the powerful benefits of meditation.*

Women's Bodies, Women's Wisdom: Creating Physical and Emotional Health and Healing by Christiane Northrup (Bantam, 1998)

> *Dr. Northrup's book on all aspects of women's health is an essential text for women of all ages.*

WEBSITES

www.centerpointe.com

> *This website contains information on Bill Harris, his books and research, and the Holosync Technology—one of the best programs I've found for deepening the experience of meditation and increasing the brain's capacity to handle stress.*

www.greatpeace.net

> *Jerry Thomas's website that contains information about his retreats, chant CDs (including the Om Sai and Jesus prayer chants) as well as other valuable resources.*

www.yogananda-srf.org

> *This website contains information on Paramahansa Yogananda as well as a variety of spiritual books, audio and video programs, chant CDs, and retreat information.*

AUDIO PROGRAMS

Devotion: Understanding Its Deeper Aspects in the Search for God by Brother Anandamoy (Self-Realization Fellowship)

> *This audiotape is about cultivating love for God and the true meaning of surrender and how it helps one to become receptive to the presence, guidance, and blessings of God.*

The Interior Life by Mrinalini Mata (Self-Realization Fellowship)

> *Using examples from the lives of saints, Mrinalini Mata (a monk from the Self-Realization Fellowship) talks about how we can create within ourselves a blessed haven of peace and Divine communion—where we find strength, solace, and clear insight for all the changes and challenges of life.*

Padre Pio Sanctus (Janson Video Inc.)

> *A biography of the saint from Pietrelcina, Italy. With more than 135 minutes of filmed material, much of which has never been seen before, this DVD introduces the faithful to every aspect of the life, spirituality, and work of this twentieth-century saint.*

Spiritual Marriage by Brother Anandamoy (Self-Realization Fellowship)

> *This is a beautiful lecture from a monk who is a direct disciple of Paramahansa Yogananda, about relationships and understanding the deeper, universal purpose of marriage.*

7

◆

EMBRACE THE BEAUTY OF LIFE

Once you conquer your mind, you have conquered the world. Once you have found joy and beauty within, the whole world becomes infused with joy and beauty. Once you are successful inside, external success is yours. Once you surrender your desires to the Almighty, you are free of your personal whims and ambitions. Then the Divine Will itself becomes your desire.

I came across this quote while reading a book called *At the Eleventh Hour* by Pandit Rajmani Tigunait, Ph.D. It's a beautiful description of how our lives change when we open ourselves to grace and make the practice of silence a daily part of our lives.

When we seize the moment that challenges us to live a more conscious life, we set in motion an awakening process that gains momentum over time. As a result, the evidence of grace that is always present in our lives becomes vivid and recognizable. Instead of seeing our experiences or encounters with others as random occurrences, we see them as deliberate, spiritual events that remind us of who we really are—magnificent souls being molded and shaped by sacred hands.

As we respond to the influence of grace we naturally begin to live a more soul-directed life. Our perspective on what it means to be truly happy matures and it becomes obvious that a satisfying life is not about making money, finding the right career, or enjoying perfect health. Instead it's about using life experiences as learning opportunities to grow and evolve as spiritual beings. As this evolution in consciousness takes place, we are continually reminded that the key to long-lasting peace and fulfillment comes from a solid connection to our spiritual core, and an intimate, on-going relationship with a Higher Power.

The process of spiritual awakening is a lifelong journey. There is no predetermined destination. We must simply build upon our relationship with a Higher Power and allow grace to lead us down our own unique spiritual paths. As we do, there are clear indications—what I call spiritual signposts—that reflect our new way of being in the world.

———◆———

As I learned to balance silence with activity, the way I lived my life started to change. When faced with uncertainty and the obsessive urge to control the outcome of a situation, I had the good sense to surrender my will to a higher order, trusting that all would happen as it should. When I felt overwhelmed by my commitments, I chose to stop and meditate to refocus my efforts instead of frantically trying to multitask my way to sanity. If my goals or plans failed to unfold the way I wanted, I still felt disappointed or discouraged, but the time I spent suffering about it gradually decreased. I stopped letting the illusion of success = true happiness run my life.

When we're receptive to the influence of grace, we experience life on a deeper level. Our senses are heightened and we feel more. Gradually we begin to appreciate the subtleties of life. We find joy in simple things and in unexpected places. The more we make silence a daily part of our lives, the less stress and tension we experience, and pretty soon we recognize that our responses to conditions, circumstances, or events start to change. What kind of spiritual signposts are you likely to notice? Here are some examples:

You have faith that all is happening as it should.

You bring the peace of silence into your everyday life.

You feel a stronger connection to all living things.

You enjoy a heightened sensitivity to beauty.

YOU HAVE FAITH THAT ALL IS HAPPENING AS IT SHOULD

In 1991 my friend Andrew had a rare opportunity to see the difference that grace made in his life. At the height of his career as a make-up artist and instructor for a major beauty company, Andrew was diagnosed with leukemia. Like many people who are suddenly faced with a serious illness, Andrew had a variety of reactions. "One minute I was angry—angry with God, myself, and the whole damn world. The next, I felt guilty about my anger. I walked around terrified most of the time, unable to eat, sleep, or even carry on a conversation. I felt like my body had betrayed me, and at the same time, I wondered how I might have caused what was happening."

After doing his best to deny the severity of his illness, Andrew finally came to terms with it. He cleaned up his diet, decreased his workload, and started praying for the first time in his life. He also began seeing an expressive arts therapist who helped him tend to his emotional health while he was undergoing chemotherapy. Three years later, Andrew was given a clean bill of health. But, this wasn't the end of his story.

In 1996, Andrew discovered that his cancer had returned. "I was stunned. I sat in the doctor's office crying as he gave me the details. I wasn't sure I had the strength to face this again. But, over the next several days, I knew exactly what I needed to do. My first bout with cancer opened my heart to a more spiritual way of life. Now I had the solid foundation I needed to deal with this setback. As I stood in my bathroom looking in the mirror, I said out loud, 'I surrender, God. I'm frightened, but I turn this situation over to you. Please help me face this challenge with courage and faith.'

"From this point on, I felt more at peace as I faced the ups and downs that are characteristic of the treatment process. During my first illness I was so angry that I treated people rather harshly. I was short-tempered, impatient, and at times, even arrogant. But this time was different. I accepted that sometimes things happen for reasons we don't understand and I was able to treat my health care providers with kindness and respect. I also allowed my family and friends to support me instead of suffering alone. I was able to trust that God was working through the people in my life and knew I had to keep this channel open.

"During my first brush with this illness, I thought *I* was in control and it made me blind to the grace that surrounded me. This time, when I let go and allowed things to unfold as they were meant to, I was surprised by how quickly my fear disappeared. Of course, there were still times when I felt scared, but this time I had faith. During the entire healing process, I focused on feeling the presence of a Higher Power. I was lucky. Today I'm cancer free and have been for seven years. As a result, I now have a much closer relationship with my loved ones and with God. And I appreciate and cherish every single moment of my life."

Putting our faith in a Higher Power is one of the most courageous steps we ever take. This action isn't a decision of the mind, it's a practice of the heart whereby through a series of small acts of letting go, we move closer and closer to the understanding that we have a limited amount of control to begin with. As grace becomes a familiar companion we naturally begin to do our part, and then surrender the outcome to Divine Will, trusting that with the strength and power of this connection we can handle whatever comes our way.

In addition to handling difficult life issues in a whole new way, opening our lives to grace makes dealing with less serious issues easier, too. My client Mandy had evidence of this while helping her children complete applications for college. Mandy admitted, "When my daughter applied to college, my husband Ken and I were obsessed with getting her into the right school. We badgered her to complete her essays, and called everyone we knew to find an in with any of the universities. It was ridiculous. I was constantly worrying about what might happen, and I tried to anticipate every possible outcome. Of course, all it did was cause me a lot of unnecessary suffering.

"Now, four years later, as we prepared for our son to go to college, I could see that all Ken and I could do was take actions that were within our power and be patient. This time around we had faith that the right school would choose our son. The process was so much easier. No struggling, no bickering, and no worrying about the end result. Although our son didn't get accepted to the school he most wanted, at the end of his freshman year, it was clear that he was given the best choice."

When we learn to balance silence with activity and strengthen our spiritual foundation, it becomes easier to release our attachment to the outcome and have faith in a higher plan. Being able to surrender not only frees us emotionally; it releases the spiritual or energetic hold we have on the events themselves, allowing the right result to occur at the right time. Whether we realize it or not, we all walk a spiritual path, one that's aligned with our soul's development. Any attempt to force or manage an outcome only disrupts this alignment. As we learn to let go, we come to understand that when things don't go our way, it's because something more important to the growth of our soul is in the works.

My friend Jonathan is a good example of a person who has learned to have faith. Over the years his spiritual reawakening led him back to the church of his youth. Jonathan became a devout Christian. When faced with a tragedy he not only survived, he thrived thanks to his faith and supportive spiritual community.

One Saturday evening while Jonathan was away with his church youth group, his home was destroyed by fire. It wasn't until the next morning, when he received a call from his friend Betsy, that he received the bad news. On his way to assess the damage with his friend Sam, Jonathan repeatedly prayed, "God, please show me what's next."

When Jonathan arrived at the scene he found that most of his possessions were either badly damaged or completely destroyed. When Sam saw this, he immediately contacted the church. Several people came to help clean up the debris. For more than four hours the group sifted through the rubble and salvaged whatever they could. When they finished, Sam invited Jonathan to stay at his house until he got back on his feet.

Jonathan said he was aware of God's presence throughout the whole painful ordeal. For example, the fire, which resulted from an electrical short, was reported to the fire department at approximately 2 AM. The report came from Jonathan's next-door neighbor who was awakened by the cries of his nine-month-old daughter. When he went to her room he noticed a flash of light and, assuming it was an ambulance, went to the window to see what was happening. To his surprise, he saw Jonathan's home on fire. He also noticed that the fire was dangerously close to his car. Fearing that it would reach the gas tank, he asked his wife to dial 911 while he ran outside to move the car away from the flames.

The following Sunday morning, once Jonathan and his friends finished salvaging what they could from the fire, they went to church. Members formed a circle around Jonathan and began to pray. They asked that he be given the support he needed during this difficult time. Following the service, Jonathan learned that a collection had been taken to help him find a new place to live. From this point on, Jonathan said he was continually blessed by God's grace as, time after time, he received exactly what he needed, exactly when he needed it.

Jonathan began by trying to find a new home. Coincidently, his chiropractic office was located on the ground level of a small apartment building. When he contacted his landlord, he was told that the apartment above his office was available. In addition, Jonathan was told he could rent the apartment at a reduced rate without a security deposit. Within forty-eight hours he had a new home.

Over the next week he received many unexpected gifts, including a microwave oven, new clothes, and toiletries. Then, after some women at his church threw him a shower to replace his kitchen supplies, his father, who owned a moving company, made arrangements to send him some used furniture. The following Saturday Jonathan had a completely furnished apartment.

Some of the most heartwarming gifts that Jonathan received took him by surprise. For example, the ten-year-old daughter of a friend gave him an envelope that contained four dollars. In it was a note that read, "I figured you could use this more than I could." It was all the money she had. Then, his brother, a forester in Oregon, sent him a collection of science fiction books (a hobby they shared), and a photo album filled with family pictures to replace those that were lost in the fire.

"Although losing my home was devastating," Jonathan said, "my faith kept me strong. I trusted that I'd receive help, but I never imagined that I'd get as much as I did, and from so many different people. Now it takes me thirty seconds to get to work, I have an entire apartment full of new furniture, and I live in a home that I love more than the one I lost. More importantly, I have so many wonderful friends who've taught me what love truly means." Jonathan finished his story by saying, "I have always asked God to give me what I needed to grow and evolve as a person. While I would never have asked for the fire, my prayers have been answered tenfold. Now I know that the greatest possession I'll ever own is my unwavering faith."

It's wonderful to be reminded that we can lean back into the arms of grace when we find ourselves faced with a challenging situation. There is no better time to feel this connection. Trusting that our lives are divinely guided gives us the courage to surrender our will and have faith that all is happening as it should.

YOU BRING THE PEACE OF SILENCE
INTO YOUR EVERYDAY LIFE

The next spiritual signpost may take you by surprise. I remember the day when I recognized the effect that meditation was having on my quality of life. I was driving to the store when I noticed that I wasn't worrying about anything. My mind was peaceful and relaxed. I suddenly realized that rather than thinking about all the work I had to do or the next trip I needed to take, I was present to the moment, enjoying the scenery and thankful for such a beautiful day. It was as though my brain kicked into neutral. As I thought about this, it felt strange. I immediately started searching for the normal ramblings of my busy mind, but they were nowhere to be found. Instead, I felt like I had a current of peace running through my veins.

While attending Jerry's retreats I heard him talk about the peace that students would experience as they made silence a part of their daily lives. I remember thinking, "I can't wait to get there!" But, even though it took a little longer than I hoped, as I continued my meditation practice, it seemed that peace had finally found me. Now I was able to maintain a healthy detachment from the goals and desires that used to beg for my attention. My choice to make silence a regular practice helped me feel less overwhelmed by the demands of life. Whether it was unfinished work, unreturned phone calls and e-mails, or making plans for my next trip, I was no longer obsessed with getting things done. Now, my doer mentality was slowly being replaced with an even-keeled, calmer state of being. As a result, the idea of working too hard to achieve a goal felt foolish and exhausting. It wasn't that I shirked my responsibilities; it's just that I no longer felt unhinged by them. The more I lived in the present moment, the less concerned I was with the step in front of me, or the one I had just taken. Now was the only place to be.

My client Monica began to notice that she was handling everyday problems in a much calmer and healthier way. One morning her car broke down on the way to work. Instead of getting angry and stewing until the tow truck arrived, Monica said she closed her eyes and took advantage of the opportunity to rest. She said, "In the past I would have had myself so worked up by the time the mechanic arrived that I would have been bitchy and rude. Instead, I decided that this was just God's way of telling me that I wasn't supposed to be at work yet."

Whether you're scrambling to get the kids ready for school, late for an important meeting, or concerned about world events, maintaining a calm, steady course can seem like a daunting task. But when you learn to balance silence with activity, you preserve your connection to grace. You learn to observe your emotional state and use it as a barometer for the quality of your thoughts. For example, when you feel upset, it's safe to assume that it's because your thoughts are negative or, in some way, unsettling. Once you become more cognizant of how your thoughts are affecting your emotional state, you can change the way you think and feel by repeating a mantra or prayer.

One day I saw an extraordinary example of how a woman was able to maintain a state of peace when faced with one of the most stressful and worrisome experiences we ever have—death. I was watching a show about death and dying on the Wisdom Channel, a television network dedicated to conscious living. The segment focused on work being done at the San Francisco-based Zen Hospice Center, founded by Frank Ostaseski. Frank was interviewing Kamli Lam, a courageous woman who was willing to share how she felt while preparing to die. She spoke with grace and elegance, and maintained a sense of calm that allowed her to face death with dignity and acceptance.

Frank explained that the peace we saw in Kamli reflected an unusually enlightened perspective of life and death. When he asked her about the dying process, she said, "To me, dying is just another piece of moving on. It's a different form of existence. It's like a butterfly. At one point you have a cocoon that eventually dies and yet gives birth to a beautiful butter- fly." Toward the end of the segment Frank asked Kamli an interesting question. "Consider this," he said, "you can have your health back, but you have to relinquish the learning and growing. What would you do?" Kamli's reply was immedi- ate. "Oh no," she said, "the learning has given me peace. It has taught me that I have God inside here (she points to her heart). That strength, that peace, that joy is invaluable . . . that love . . . that's what life is all about."

YOU FEEL A STRONGER CONNECTION
TO ALL LIVING THINGS

When we live a spiritually based life and cultivate the pres- ence of grace, we begin to understand, on a fundamental level, that we are each a vital part of a greater whole. We begin to see the divinity in all living things. When grace opens our hearts, we feel more connected to the people in our community, our state, and throughout the world. We also feel more connected to the natural world, from the smallest insect to the largest tree. Appreciating this connec- tion makes us feel more responsible for preserving and respecting all forms of life. It makes us care more about what happens to the environment, or supporting those in need. Our actions become more conscious and life affirming. We're inspired to clean up our communities, stay informed about political issues, or get involved in projects that help others have a better quality of life.

As I developed a stronger sense of this connection, I became more conscious of my actions. For example, while in the past, I thought nothing of killing a spider when I found one on my bedroom wall, I now felt compelled to place it outdoors. I felt protective of the land and could no longer use pesticides or weed killer on my lawn. Not only was I concerned for my family, but for my neighbors as well. I also became deeply affected by world events. A tragedy in a country on the other side of the globe was no longer something that happened "over there." People from all races, religions, or ethnic backgrounds were members of a larger family called humanity.

This feeling of interconnectedness manifests itself in different ways for different people. For example, Norma, a member of our online community, had a powerful experience that made her feel more connected to nature. Here's her story:

"Years ago, at a time when I was trying to heal from the abuse I suffered as a child, I decided to spend some time in Alaska with my older brother. One weekend we hiked several miles to a very remote, mountainous area called the Chugach Mountain range. After several hours, we set up camp in a basin, near a beautiful pond. Circling above us were two eagles hunting for fish and animals. In the distance we could see beavers building a dam and a moose running through the woods. My brother sat down to read a book, while I felt compelled to climb one of the nearby mountains.

"As I began my trek I immediately found myself think-

ing about the abuse I'd experienced as a child. While climbing, I wondered how I'd ever move past it and if there was
anything I could do to accelerate the process. I wanted desperately to find the peace to move on with my life.

"As I made my way up the rough terrain, I imagined
that climbing alone was symbolic of my lone struggle to
heal. With this in mind, I was determined to make it to the
top. The climb was much steeper and more grueling than I
anticipated. Soon I began to lose my breath. The climb had
become so difficult that it brought tears to my eyes. I had to
rest after every few steps. My legs were burning and the air
was thin, but something kept making me move. If I can
reach the top of this mountain, I thought, there isn't anything I can't overcome.

"At this point I was exhausted, but even more determined. With every step, I imagined that I was overcoming
the pain of my past. Finally, after what seemed like forever, I
arrived at the top of the mountain. When I looked down, I
could barely see my brother. There was a narrow footpath
on the upper ridge of the mountain and as I looked off into
the distance, I could see the craggy ridges of mountaintops
off in the distance capped with snow. It was absolutely silent.

"As I stood alone on the narrow ridge of the summit, the
beauty was like nothing I had ever witnessed before. Then,
as I sat on the ridge top, basking in my accomplishment, I
suddenly noticed a rainbow in the basin below. I immediately
felt butterflies in my stomach. Then, as I continued to stare at
the rainbow, two more formed! Now I was the lone witness
to three incredible rainbows! I started to cry tears of joy.

"While I would have enjoyed sharing this experience
with my brother, I had the feeling that at this moment, I was

the only person meant to see this extraordinary sight. I felt I had *earned* this moment, and that it was a gift from God. Suddenly I felt a profound connection to life—to the mountains, the rainbows, the animals, and my brother. I also understood how climbing the mountain was a metaphor for how I needed to deal with my fear and work through the pain. I could have what I wanted if I faced the truth and committed to staying the course. I also realized that, contrary to what I once thought, I did not have to do it alone. For me, this was an important revelation. I'll never forget it."

We are never alone. As we develop a relationship with the sacred dimension of life we realize we are but one small part of an interconnected whole.

My client Amanda felt a greater connection to a Higher Power when experiencing what she called bliss moments, sudden feelings of deep gratitude for everything in her life. "These moments often occur with no particular rhyme or reason," she said. "For example, I might be standing in line at the post office, driving in my car, or talking with a friend on the phone. Typically, I'm overcome by a feeling of great joy. And while my heart swells with love, my eyes fill with tears. In these moments I feel more compassionate toward others and aware of my surroundings. At the most unexpected times, and in the most unexpected places, I find myself saying, Thank you God, for this amazing gift of life."

I've had experiences that are similar to Amanda's moments of bliss, and for me, they've occurred not only when I've felt content with life, but also when I've felt distressed. For example, when I first decided to write this book I felt torn about whether to share personal stories from my life. Although I was used to sharing my stories with audiences, I felt more exposed putting them on paper. One day, as I drove to my office, going back and forth in my mind about whether it was the right thing to do, "The Book of My Life," a song by Sting, came on the radio. It spoke about the conflict and vulnerability he experienced while writing his memoir. I immediately felt that this song was meant for me—to inspire me to tell the truth. The synchronicity of this moment also reminded me that I wasn't the only one writing this book. Every step of the way, God would be guiding my hand.

I'm sure you've had your own moments of bliss. You open a book to a passage that is just what you need to hear, and you feel comforted by the timeliness of its message. Or, you have an intimate conversation with a friend and you silently offer a prayer of thanks for having that person in your life. These types of moments enable a deeper and more powerful connection with others, one where we are no longer strangers, but a necessary and special part of each other's lives.

I recall a very personal example of this during a train ride to New York. It was the first anniversary of September 11 and I was scheduled to be in Manhattan. My husband accompanied me on the trip and as we sat on the train eating breakfast, the conductor announced that there would be a minute of silence in recognition of those who lost their lives in the tragedy. I braced myself, anticipating a very emotional reaction.

When the bell marked the beginning of the silence I started to cry. As the tears ran down my cheeks, I felt exposed so I covered my face with my hands. When I finally looked up, a woman seated a few rows from us smiled at me with a look that said, "I'm right here with you. Don't feel embarrassed, I know just how you feel." She held my gaze for several seconds and in that brief moment I could see the connection I felt to her and to everyone who was affected by September 11 reflected in her eyes.

YOU ENJOY A HEIGHTENED
SENSITIVITY TO BEAUTY

"The capacity to perceive God's beauty and goodness around us," Paramahansa Yogananda says, "is one of the joys that accompanies the gradual awakening of self-realization—and one of the signs of spiritual maturity." One of the most pleasurable aspects of being open to grace is a heightened sensitivity to beauty. As I see it, beauty is the language of the Divine. The more we feel connected to the oneness of all things, the more we tune in to the world around us. The practice of silence teaches us to be present. When we are, our senses are greatly enhanced. One day while at the beach I had an experience of this heightened awareness. As I closed my eyes and relaxed in the warm sun, I heard an unusual sound. I opened my eyes and looked up to see a seagull circling overhead waiting for food. The sound was the gentle waft of air being made by its wings. I thought to myself, I've sat on the beach thousands of times and never noticed that sound before.

Over the years, many of my clients have reported an increased awareness of simple pleasures as they've slowed down to live more spiritually balanced lives. When we do, even the most mundane aspects of everyday life turn out to be some of the most satisfying experiences we have. For example, there have been times when I felt like I could stare for hours at the bird feeder in my backyard, watching tiny yellow finches dance in the air, vying for a spot on a perch. A simple treat like this feels like food for the soul. As my friend Taylor said, "Before I decided to live consciously I'd drive to and from work barely noticing anything. Now, as I drive home along the river, it's not uncommon for me to pull over and sit by the water's edge. I just stare at the soft, peach colored hues of the late afternoon sun reflected on the water and I think to myself, '*This* is what life's all about.'"

Grace turns up the volume on all of our senses. Whether we find pleasure relaxing in a warm bath, delighting in the touch of a baby's hand, or enjoying the gentle tinkling of chimes as they sway in the wind, we start to see that, aside from the necessities of living, much of what brings us joy can be found in the milieu of our daily lives. While discussing this with a group of women during a workshop, one said, "I know exactly what you mean. One night I came downstairs to get a glass of water. I passed by my office, glanced out the window, and saw moonlight reflected on the snow covering our lawn. It looked like someone had placed a silver-colored, velvet comforter over the ground. I walked into the dark room, sat down in a chair by the window and stayed there for a while looking out at this surreal image. I was brought to tears. But it wasn't just the beauty that did it. It was the realization that I was beginning to see my life, truly see it, in a way I never had before."

There is amazing spiritual energy in the natural world. Clients of all faiths and traditions have, at one time or another, said that feeling this energy has strengthened their faith. For example, my client Rachel said that during a time in her life when she was having financial problems, she made a point to get up early to watch the sunrise. She would drive to a local park near her home in southern Texas, and sit quietly on a bench near some beautiful farmland. Rachel said that watching the extraordinary beauty of the sunrise gave her a feeling of abundance and deep gratitude for the gifts of the natural world. It also helped her put her financial fears into perspective. While she didn't have much money, knowing that she always had access to a wealth of beauty in nature made her feel rich nonetheless.

My client Melissa said that she too had become more aware of nature's beauty. She said, "I live in the northeast. One morning after a snowfall, I went cross-country skiing in a forest near my home. As I glided along the trail between lines of tall pine trees, I stopped to take in the scenery and experience the hushed silence of the snow-covered landscape. There was something primal in my response to what I saw. I suddenly felt protected by these tall, majestic trees lined up like sturdy soldiers on either side of my path. They seemed to have an energy that I could really feel! Today, a date with nature heads my list of things to do."

So often, as clients make their inner life more of a priority, they feel a need to move closer to the natural world. Some choose to move to a new geographical location. Others move on to a new line of work, one that affords them time to enjoy doing things outdoors. The stress and noise of a busy life in a crowded community are in direct conflict with their increasing sensitivity, and they are no longer willing to sacrifice their desire for beauty. Instead, it

becomes a major source of energy and joy. And, it provides
a vital connection to the Divine.

———◆———

In the spring, my period of rest was coming to an end as I
prepared to travel again. Now that I had begun to see the
spiritual signposts in my own life, I wondered if it was realistic to expect that I could return to a full work schedule
and still maintain the way of life that I had grown to love
and appreciate. I wanted to continue to write and teach, but
at the same time, I wanted the space to stay connected to
nature, my spiritual practices, and my inner life. Until this
point, though, I still hadn't found a role model who had
successfully learned how to balance work life with a fulfilling spiritual life. But during a trip to California, this all
changed.

In April of 2003 I traveled to Los Angeles on business.
Having come from a previous engagement in Arizona, I
scheduled a few days off in between to relax and to make a
special visit to the international headquarters of the Self-
Realization Fellowship (SRF) center founded by Paramahansa Yogananda. During my studies of mystical spirituality I had read about his life in *The Autobiography of a Yogi,*
and was now studying his translation of the *Bhagavad-Gita.*
Both books had left a powerful impression on me, and I was
curious to see where this great man had lived and taught.

One month before my trip, I had a conversation with
Jerry and told him about my plans to visit the center. He
suggested that I call to see if I might schedule a meeting
with one of the nuns. Jerry gave me the name of a special
woman—an ordained minister in her eighties whom many

considered a living saint—someone who is immersed in God's communion. Jerry said that while it was highly unlikely that I'd be able to speak to her, I should at least give it a try. I remember his final words, "Say a prayer. If it's God's will, you'll get to see her."

As soon as I finished talking to Jerry, I dialed the center's main line. I asked to be connected to the woman he mentioned and was put on hold. After several minutes, I was greeted by a sweet, almost childlike voice inquiring about my needs. When I said who I wanted to speak with, she promptly informed me that she *was* that person. "Well," I thought to myself, "I guess I am supposed to speak with her."

I stood motionless at my desk unsure of what to say next. Several seconds passed and I finally acknowledged my surprise at being connected with her directly. She replied, "Well my dear, it is quite unusual. How might I help you?" I explained my interest in visiting the center and my desire to meet with her while there. After listening patiently as I stumbled over my words, she told me that she would have her secretary set up a meeting.

As I prepared for my trip, I had a last-minute change in my plans. I was presented with an opportunity to host a national television show. Although I had turned down television offers after my series on the Oxygen Network, this time the invitation was for a full-time position with a major network. Although I wanted a few days off, I felt like I needed to give it serious consideration, so I agreed to a meeting when I arrived in LA.

The day after I arrived in Los Angeles I headed for SRF headquarters. On my way there, I chatted with my driver, feeling excited about my visit. The center was located on the top of Mt. Washington, and as we climbed the narrow, winding road, I admired the view. When our car reached the entrance, I was immediately struck by the beauty and tranquility of this incredible mountainside sanctuary. As soon as we passed through the giant gates, my eyes filled with tears. The energy or vibration of this place was palpable. In that instant I had an overwhelming feeling that I needed to cancel my meeting about the television show. For some reason I couldn't explain, I knew that a national show was not something I was meant to do at this time. There was no second-guessing or hesitation whatsoever. I felt certain that the answer was "no."

My driver parked the car by a small garden and as I walked toward the entrance of the building I stopped to take in the view. There were big, ancient trees, many small benches perfectly placed throughout the grounds for quiet contemplation, and flower gardens everywhere. When I entered the building, it felt like I'd entered a church. The hushed silence felt comforting and familiar. I went to the front desk, announced my arrival, and was asked to wait in the chapel.

Several minutes later I was directed to a room at the top of a grand staircase. As I slowly climbed the steps I wondered, "What do you say to a saint? How should I greet her?" When I arrived at the top of the stairs I was met by a silver-haired woman with bright, sparkling blue eyes. She was beautiful and looked to be in her sixties. The moment I came within a few feet of her, I felt a sense of calmness wash over me, as if I had stepped under a gentle shower of light. It suddenly hit me—I was in the company of grace.

For the next hour we talked about a variety of topics—architecture, nature, and our shared love of beauty and its importance to one's soul. She was funny and wise, and had a mischievous quality that I found quite amusing. Her very essence was love itself and while it was obvious that she had a sharp, discerning eye, she held no judgment, only genuine compassion for all souls struggling to find their way in the world.

It is said that a saint or true spiritual teacher can elevate the consciousness of another human being. As I left our meeting that day I felt changed on a very deep level. While I learned a lot during our conversation, it wasn't her words that had the most impact on me. It was her company. She didn't need to offer any profound wisdom or bestow any special blessings. *Her presence was her message.*

Later that afternoon, I remembered something Jerry once said during a retreat, "One saint can do more good for the planet than a thousand do-gooders." After my meeting I understood why. Over the next several months, as I continued to integrate my experience on Mt. Washington, I knew that it was as important for me to maintain my daily practice of meditation and prayer as it was any part of my business. And I learned that to make my most meaningful contribution to others, my presence would have to be my message.

When I left the center that day I called my contact for the television show and withdrew my interest. I knew in my heart that something more important was on the horizon and I wanted to have the space in my life to welcome it with open arms. Now, the kind of offers and opportunities that were once so attractive were no longer that important. I was finding my "enough."

Experiment: Finding Your Spiritual Signposts

This experiment is designed to increase your awareness of how your life is changing as you awaken to grace. Using your journal, answer the following questions that relate to each signpost. Take your time when considering examples and be sure to include small changes as well. Here are the four signposts to consider:

1. *You have faith that all is happening as it should.*

    Think of a recent event where you chose to have faith rather than control the outcome. What specifically did you do to keep your faith alive? Who supported your efforts? How did your decision to have faith benefit you?

2. *You bring the peace of silence into your everyday life.*

    For the next week, make it a point to *observe* the way you react and respond to normal everyday occurrences. Are you handling challenges any differently? Are you able to have a more peaceful and centered response to situations that used to push your buttons? What new behaviors do you notice?

3. *You feel a stronger connection to all living things.*

    In what ways are you more aware of being connected to all living things? Have you made any changes that take into account the needs of others? How have your relationships changed? Do you feel a stronger connection to the planet, nature, or to others?

4. *You enjoy a heightened sensitivity to beauty.*

    In what ways have your senses been heightened? Are you more aware of the beauty that surrounds you? What kinds of things have you started to notice that you were oblivious to before? Make a list of the aesthetic qualities that you value. What changes have you made to honor the beauty in your life?

Resources

BOOKS

At the Eleventh Hour by Pandit Rajmani Tigunait, Ph.D. (Himalayan Institute, 2001)

> *A fascinating story of Swami Rama, a modern day mystic, social entrepreneur, yogi, scholar, and musician.*

Autobiography of a Yogi by Paramahansa Yogananda (Self-Realization Fellowship, 1998)

> *A master storyteller, Yogananda introduces the reader to Eastern spiritual thought through the story of his amazing life.*

The Second Coming of Christ by Paramahansa Yogananda (Self-Realization Fellowship, 2004)

> *This book takes the reader on a journey through the four gospels and the teachings of Christ, providing people of all faiths with the means to know God. It is a full-color book with sepia duotone prints of Christ's life.*

When the Trees Say Nothing: Writings on Nature by Thomas Merton, edited by Kathleen Deignan and drawings by John Guiliani (Sorin Books, 2003)

> *A compilation of Merton's writings on the beauty of nature grouped thematically into sections on the seasons, elements, creatures, and other topics.*

Women of Power and Grace by Timothy Conway, Ph.D. (The Wake Up Press, 1994)

An amazing book about the life stories of nine female saints who perform miracles and share profound spiritual teachings with the world.

MAGAZINES

Self-Realization

A magazine devoted to the healing of body, mind, and soul.

8

◆

BECOME A SPIRITUAL PIONEER

At any moment in time, the gift of grace is available to each and every one of us. The more conscious we are of its presence, the more we recognize our own ability to be a conduit of grace for others. We become spiritual pioneers, courageous and generous souls who lead by example and feel compelled to give something back.

As we come to the end of our journey, I offer you several examples of how I, clients, and loved ones have chosen to be a source of grace in the world. But, before I do, always remember that the most effective way to share the gift of grace is to invest in your own spiritual health. Your commitment to live consciously and responsibly will continue to raise your level of consciousness, which can't help but inspire and serve as a model for those whose lives you touch.

◆

One of the best ways to share the gift of grace is to perform a simple act of kindness. Unconditional acts of kindness have the power to raise the consciousness of the receiver (as well as the giver). For example, a woman without a place to live may have an increased sense of self-worth after receiving love and attention from a volunteer at a women's shelter. Or, when a man becomes a Big Brother, his influence and guidance may redirect the course of a young man's life.

My friend Nancy received an unexpected gift of kindness that helped her save the money she needed to buy a new home. Nancy and her husband Chris had rented the same apartment for more than eight years. They dreamt of owning their own home, but the high cost of living in their community, a tourist town, made one impossible to afford. Everything they looked at was out of their price range. Their landlords, on the other hand, were fortunate to have owned investment property for over twenty-five years. After paying off the mortgage on the apartment building where Nancy and Chris lived, they decided to keep the rent low as a gesture of thanks and support for their longtime tenants.

After eight years of searching, Nancy and Chris finally found a home they could afford. Then, on their last day at their apartment they received a housewarming gift with a note that read, "My husband and I have looked forward to this day for a long time. We've enjoyed having you as tenants and we're thrilled that you've found a new home." After reading the note, Nancy said, "I had a very strong sense that they had been helping us out all along. Their concern about our financial situation (and their decision to not increase our rent) was a wonderful act of kindness. It not only allowed us to buy our first home, it brought Chris and me closer, made us feel like welcomed members of the community, and inspired us to give something back. It gave us a deeper appreciation for the effect our actions have on the lives of those around us."

Sometimes we can be a conduit for grace by helping a friend have faith in a Higher Power when he feels frightened or unsure of himself. Or, we can help by having faith *for* him until he achieves a state of spiritual balance. This might mean encouraging him to surrender when a situation is clearly out of his hands. You can do this by offering an example of how letting go made a difference in your life. It may even mean helping someone understand that a Higher Power is not just an abstract concept.

Early in my relationship with my husband Michael, we had a conversation about receiving Divine support in times of need. We discussed some of the things I've shared with you in this book. One night, we sat together reading stories about real-life "angel interventions" from *A Book of Angels* by Sophy Burnham. When we finished reading the stories I asked Michael if he believed in angels. "I'm not sure," he replied. "I'd need some kind of proof. A personal experience would help—something so clear and unmistakable that I couldn't deny it really happened." So I suggested that he ask for a sign. "Just for fun," I said, "let's ask for undeniable proof that angels really do exist." With that I took his hand and said, "We ask that Michael be given a clear sign that angels are *real* and that a Higher Power is supporting him in his search for the truth."

Michael smiled and squeezed my hand. "Thanks, hon," he said. "And now if you'll excuse me, I must prepare for my revelation." With that, he left the room and went to turn on the TV. Then, when he couldn't find anything to watch, he shut if off and pulled a magazine out of a large pile on the floor. It was then that Michael said, "Cheryl, come here. I can't believe this. Look what I just pulled out from the middle of this pile!" Michael handed me a magazine. On the cover was a drawing of an angel. But, what was even more remarkable was the artist's signature, just below the image. It read Gerrish, Michael's last name. "Well," he said, "I guess I got my sign."

BRINGING GRACE TO WORK

After my visit at the Self-Realization center, I kept my promise to make meditation, prayer, and spiritual study a more consistent part of my life. As it turned out, she was an important spiritual change agent, and our meeting inspired me to integrate my spiritual and professional life in a more thoughtful and deliberate way. I started watching for signs of grace while speaking and coaching and, at times, brought the subject up in conversations. It didn't take long for me to see that when I did, people were influenced in amazing ways.

One of the first times that I spoke about grace at a public event was in Dallas, shortly after I began writing this book. I told a story about how grace had influenced my life and invited the audience to share some of their own examples. As people revealed their experiences everyone felt moved and inspired, and by the end of the evening, there were miracles occurring all around the room.

After the talk, I stayed to sign books. As I made my way to the book signing table, I overheard people talking about the insights they received and how they felt drawn to connect with others. At one point, a woman stepped up to the table and said, "I've been looking for someone to invest in an idea I've had for a business and just met a woman who seems very interested. In fact, my idea is right up her alley. We have the same background and very similar goals!"

The next woman in line said, "I just ran into my best friend from high school. We've haven't spoken in ten years! I can't believe that she's here tonight. We're going out for a drink to catch up. What a coincidence!" When a third woman approached me I knew something was up. When I asked her why she was crying she said, "My husband has Alzheimer's. I've been doing my best to care for him at home, but I'm not sure whether I'm giving him what he really needs. Last night, as I lay in bed obsessing about what to do, I asked God to give me a sign. Tonight I met a woman who is in the *exact same situation!* She's offered to share her experience and provide me with resources. It's hard to believe. I feel like my prayer has been answered."

After two or three more examples, I realized that simply talking about grace made people more open to its influence. Suddenly, it seemed as though we were all wrapped in a cloak of spiritual energy. Important connections were being made.

That night taught me something. By creating the space to talk about grace with people who resonated with its message, it helped raise the level of consciousness in the room. This created an opening for a higher level of Divine intervention.

I left that event feeling more at home with my decision to let my spiritual life play a more prominent role in my work. And, I had a sense that this experience marked the beginning of a new chapter in my life.

SELFLESS SERVICE

To become a spiritual pioneer means becoming a more conscious spiritual change agent. In this role, your contribution can take many forms. One way of contributing is through what's called selfless service. According to the ancient philosophy of Vedanta, selfless service is called karma yoga, the path of selfless work, wherein every action is offered to God as a sacrament. By doing so, it is said that one eventually attains union with God. Jesus had a similar message. When he said, "Inasmuch as ye have done it unto the least of these my brethren, ye have done it unto me," he was making it clear, among other things, that any service offered to another was a direct offering to God.

My sister Donna had an experience that was a profound example of selfless service. In 1997 her neighbor Peggy was diagnosed with cancer. Peggy was married and had two young children, a boy age thirteen and a girl age ten. Because her husband was having a difficult time coping with her illness, Donna stepped in to offer support.

The dying process is as unique and complex as each individual human being. As someone who has sat at the bedside of both clients and loved ones who were in the final stages of their lives, I know that it can be a positive, life-altering experience if approached with open-heartedness and honest, direct communication. Unfortunately, many of us are ill-prepared for a conscious ending of a loved one's life. Instead, we often choose to stay in denial as a way to protect ourselves and to cope with the pain.

Donna was truly a gift of grace to Peggy. She visited her

almost every day, cooked meals for the kids, spent as much time with Peggy and her children as possible, and provided the resources Peggy needed to minimize her emotional and physical pain. More importantly, Donna listened. She took on the role of a silent witness, and allowed Peggy to share her fear, anger, and agonizing despair at not being able to see her children grow up. Donna didn't try to take away her pain or fix the situation. Instead, she remained present, as a witness to what Peggy needed to share. By not having an agenda, Donna was able to hold the space for a Higher Power to intervene.

As the time drew near for Peggy to say her final good-byes, Donna (a mother herself) suggested that she write a letter to each of her children. Donna thought it was important for Peggy to write some of the things she'd never get to say. She also wanted to be sure that Peggy's children had a sense of who their mother was while she was alive. At first, Peggy resisted the idea for obvious reasons—it seemed too final and painful. But then, as she became weaker, she agreed that the time was right.

To make the process easier, Donna asked Peggy to complete a series of simple statements, things like "What I love most about you is . . . What I remember most about you is . . . What I'm sorry for is . . . What I dream for you is . . .," and so on. As Peggy completed each sentence, Donna carefully took notes. When they were finished, Peggy fell asleep. Later, Donna put the letters into a special package she would give to Peggy's children when they were old enough to understand and appreciate what she had to say. She admitted, "It was one of the hardest and most important things I've ever done."

Peggy's willingness to allow Donna to participate in such an intimate process was an incredible gift of grace, too. "Now I cherish my children even more," Donna admitted. "I used to get tired listening to my two boys talk about the details of what happened at school. Now, I listen closely to every word. I was also inspired to change careers. For years I dreamt of working in sales but I was never willing to take the leap. Peggy's death made me realize that I was wasting precious time and talent by not pursuing my dreams."

The path of selfless service connects us to other human beings in a primal way. Every day we're faced with opportunities to perform simple acts of service. To recognize these opportunities, we just need to pay attention. Whether you spend ten dollars on an anonymous gift of food for a needy family or put in a good word for a coworker who's being considered for a promotion, selfless service is an act of love. Ondrea Levine, coauthor of *Who Dies?* and a woman who has dedicated her life to service, says, "Service is great work for opening our hearts and feeling more a part of the human race."

There is a sweet story told by Peter Catches in his book, *Sacred Fireplace: Life and Teachings of a Lakota Medicine Man,* that demonstrates the value of selfless service in everyday life. This story is less about the details and more about the spirit of kindness behind it.

"My uncle taught me about pride in the Lakota people and about traditional ways. Long after the kerosene lamp was blown out at night, he would ask me, 'Tunska (nephew), are you awake?' And I would say, 'Yes.' Then he would begin talking about the things that came to his mind, the things that were good for me to do. He said, 'When you walk along to the neighbors on an errand, as you walk along the creek and there is a stick of wood, perhaps six or seven feet long, you break off the other branches and carry that. When you come upon another one, you break off the branches and carry the length of it. You carry two or three, and when you arrive at the neighbor's on whatever errand you are on, take it to the woodpile. If you see an axe there, chop these branches to the length of a cooking stove, carry them inside, and place them beside the stove. When you take a dipperful of water to drink, if you see the water is getting low—usually there are two buckets there, maybe sometimes three—you take the one that has less water in it, pour it into another bucket, go outside to the barrel or the pump and bring in a bucketful for the household. In doing these small things, even though you are not told to do so, these people will be kind to you.'"

SPONTANEOUS ACTS OF GRACE

We also manifest grace when we respond to a spontaneous urge to reach out to another human being. When my client Dylan was in his mid-twenties, he was employed as the fitness director for a large health club in Arizona. Every day hundreds of people would come to the gym. Among them was a woman named Pat, who was different than most members. She never wore gym clothes, rarely talked to others, or barely even smiled for that matter. Most of the staff considered her to be unfriendly and a bit eccentric so they usually avoided her.

One evening, while closing down the gym, Dylan found

Pat on a machine hurrying to finish her routine. Aware of the staff's attitude toward her, he decided to do something different.

He appoached her, put his hand on her shoulder, and said, "Hey Pat, how are you doing today?" Pat looked up at him with a big smile and said, "I've been a member here for five years and you're the first person to show any interest in me. Thank you, it means a lot."

That one brief encounter shifted Pat's attitude completely. Dylan said, "From that day forward she entered the gym with a smile on her face. She seemed friendlier, more interested in interacting with others, and she never passed me without saying hello. My decision to approach her was such a simple gesture, yet to her it made all the difference in the world. All she needed was for someone to give her a little attention. What a lesson! Now I wonder how often I pass by people just like her and miss out on the chance to have the same kind of impact."

My friend Rosemary, a therapist for more than thirty years, was surprised by a former client. Rosemary explained, "On my birthday I took the morning off to be by myself so I could reflect on the past year and my direction for the next. I was turning sixty-five and feeling pretty good about myself. I was healthy, my marriage was strong, and I loved my work. It was a time of celebration that was further enhanced by a sweet card I received from a client I had worked with many years before. Her message read, 'I want you to know that even though we haven't worked together in over twenty years, I still think about you. Your smart advice, keen insight, and loving way of listening made such a difference in my life. When I feel stuck or unsure of what to do next, I often find myself asking: What would Rosemary do in this situation? So, this morning, when I caught myself asking that very question, I decided to send you a card. I wanted you to know how much you've influenced my life in a positive way.'"

When Rosemary read the card she said, "I was so touched by her message (and the timeliness of it) that I left it on my desk. For several days I read it over and over again. Her thoughtfulness was such a blessing. At a time in my life when I was becoming more mindful of the legacy that I would leave to others, her note was confirmation that I had made an important contribution to another human being's life. It was quite a birthday gift!"

We may never know the impact that a spontaneous gesture can have on another person. For example, the few extra moments you spend talking with the man on the corner who sells you your morning paper might provide him with the only opportunity he'll ever have to brag about his daughter who graduated from college with honors. Sometimes one small comment can be the balm that soothes a wounded heart. For example, one afternoon, while my friend Ava was minding her two small kids and pushing a carriage full of groceries at the supermarket, a woman praised her for being so patient with her children. "I have such admiration for the commitment that motherhood demands," she said. "Those children are lucky to have you for a mom!"

Ava said the comment couldn't have come at a better time. "I'd been beating myself up all week for being irritable and impatient with the kids. At the time that this woman approached me, I was feeling very impatient with my son. The fact that a stranger showed up out of nowhere and praised me for the very thing I was berating myself for reminded me to be more compassionate with myself. I needed to acknowledge what I was doing right, instead of focusing on what I was doing wrong."

My client James was on his way to lunch when he ran into a delivery man who said that his dog had unexpectedly wandered off. The man had been looking for him for over an hour and was clearly very upset. James decided to skip lunch and help him search for the dog. An hour later they returned to the man's truck only to find that the dog had come back on his own. James said, "This big broad-shouldered guy actually put his arms around me and said, 'Thank you so much. You don't know how helpful it was to have someone with me during this ordeal.' I had no idea that such a simple act would touch another person so deeply."

SHOWING UP FOR OTHERS

Being a source of grace for someone doesn't need to be an expensive or time-consuming experience. Sometimes the most important contribution we make to others is to simply show up. When you're present to life you pay attention. You listen to your daughter instead of tuning her out, or you have the sensitivity to notice when a coworker needs your support. My client Sonia said that her decision to drive two hours to attend a funeral for her former hair stylist's husband meant so much to her that she still talks about it five years later. My client Melanie said that she was surprised by the reaction of a new neighbor who cried when she delivered a pot of soup as a gesture to welcome her to the community. As simple as it sounds, sometimes just showing up can be the most powerful form of grace there is, especially during pivotal times in our lives.

Robert Johnson, Jungian analyst and author of numerous books on masculine and feminine psychology, tells a story in his memoir, *Balancing Heaven and Earth: A Memoir of Visions, Dreams, and Realization.* It's about a tradition in India that is a striking example of what it means to show up and be present for another human being. Several years ago, during a trip to India, Robert ended up in the oldest and poorest part of Calcutta where it's not unusual to see dead bodies in the street. While trying to find a hotel, Robert had an amazing experience:

> I managed to find a rickshaw driver to pull me around, but I had no luck in finding another hotel. Each street that we turned down seemed to be worse than the last, until I became inundated with the darkness and the agony of India. It became more than I could cope with, so I got out of the rickshaw to walk for a while. In the next block, a woman dressed in filthy, tattered clothes pushed a dead baby into my arms while begging for money. Next I encountered small children poking me with amputated arms and withered legs. I couldn't find a building that looked safe, and I began to lose my composure. I was one

thousand miles from anyone I knew and felt myself falling into an abyss. It was worse than a panic attack; it was as if I had wandered into some corner of hell.

Then I remembered that there was something to do. I had once been told by a friend that in India you have the right to approach a stranger and ask that person to be the incarnation of God. It is a startling custom in Indian religious life where one may approach another person—man, woman, old, young, known, unknown—and ask that person such a profoundly religious question. This person may refuse the request, but generally it is considered a sacred duty to accept the role if he or she possibly can because it is an honor and such a profound experience. From that time on, the adored person will be treated like God and will be revered as if God were present in the form of that person.

Luckily I had tucked away my knowledge of this custom somewhere in the back of my brain. I could see trees off in the distance, and I walked several more blocks until I reached a tiny park. Then I began desperately looking for someone I could approach and ask to be my incarnation of God. I spotted a middle-aged man; he was dressed in Indian fashion and was barefoot, but he had an air of dignity and calmness. I am amazed now at my boldness, but I was driven by desperation. I approached him.

"Sir, do you speak English?"

"Yes."

"Would you be the incarnation of God for me?"

"Yes," he replied, without losing his dignity at my extraordinary request.

It is a staggering thought that he would understand and accept this; all I had to do was ask the question. He pointed me to a bench, and for the next twenty minutes I poured out my woes, telling him who I was and how Calcutta had worn me down, that I felt as if I would soon disintegrate. He said not a word but listened patiently to me. I continued to lay out this burden that was too much for me to experience by myself, and gradually I began to feel calmer. It was as if the burden halved in sharing it with him, and half of it I could cope with. He really didn't have to say a word, just listen to me, and that is what he did. Eventually I regained my wits; I wasn't happy, but I could function again. As soon as I could, I thanked him, at which point he stood up and bowed. I was afraid he was about to walk off and remain a total stranger forever, so I blurted out, "Please tell me something about yourself—who are you?"

He told me his name, which I cannot now recall. It was unpronounceable to me.

"Yes, thank you," I said, "but who are you in life, what is your work?"

"I am a Roman Catholic priest," he replied, plainly and directly.

I was speechless. Amid millions of people swarming Calcutta I had tapped a Catholic priest on the shoulder and asked if he would be the incarnation of God for me. There are not that many Catholics in Calcutta and very few priests, yet I had somehow picked him out to hear my confession. Now I had nothing more to say. I thanked him and bowed, and he bowed back with quiet dignity, then he turned and walked away. I have never forgotten that man, and I suspect that he never forgot me.

A GATHERING OF GRACE

Sue Little was inspired to be a conduit for grace in her community by bringing a group of Tibetan monks to her bookstore, Jabberwocky Books. A friend told her that the monks were traveling throughout the United States leading mediation groups. They were from the Sera Je monastery in India and were trying to raise money for their community. A year earlier Sue had had a powerful healing experience during a meditation workshop, and when she heard about the monks coming to the United States, she made a decision to return the gift by bringing them to her bookstore.

Sue set aside a room for the monks to create a mandala sand painting—a sacred work of art that consists of millions of grains of colored sand meticulously laid into place on a flat platform. This work of art was created over several days and while the monks worked, members of the community came to watch. Once the mandala was finished, customers were invited to a ceremony designed to symbolize the impermanence of life, whereby the monks would empty their creation into the ocean so the water could carry its healing energies into the world.

Along with the creation of the mandala, every night the

monks led a group meditation where anyone from the community could come to enjoy an hour of silence. People from all faiths and spiritual backgrounds joined together to meditate with one another. The event was a huge success. It created a spiritual buzz in town that had people talking for weeks. It was also a financial success. Members of the community raised more than $20,000!

Every year, between Christmas and New Year's, I hold a special gathering in my home to celebrate the spiritual traditions of loved ones. I invite ten friends for dinner and each guest is asked to bring a gift that holds some kind of spiritual significance. It might be a small object that nurtures the spirit, an item that represents a religious practice, or a talisman that has provided courage during a difficult time.

The gift exchange allows each guest to share his or her unique spiritual beliefs in a safe and supportive environment. The presents are lined up in a row and numbered. Then, each guest pulls a slip of paper from a hat, and once the person with number one has chosen a gift, we then move on to number two, and so forth. When everyone has finished, we open the gifts, one by one, and as the contents are revealed, the giver explains its spiritual significance.

It is always amazing to see the miraculous way that the appropriate gift ends up in the right person's hand. For example, my friend Jonathan received a photo of the Grand Canyon taken by another guest (someone he had never met) who loves to hike and ride her mountain bike in beautiful natural settings. Jonathan is an avid mountain biker who dreams of riding in Utah and Arizona. I chose to give several pieces of sea glass, a special seashell, and one of my favorite prayers. I wrapped them all up in long strips of red tulle, tied together to form a starfish. These items represented my spiritual connection with the ocean. My friend Peter chose my gift and when he opened it, we discovered a shared passion for collecting sea glass and seashells. Unbeknownst to me, Peter had been collecting both for more than twenty-five years.

This annual gathering is designed to create a mood and environment that encourages deeper conversations about how the Divine affects our lives. The stories are intimate. Because the gifts represent a special and often private aspect of the giver's life, we often learn things about each other that we never knew. The evening has become a very important part of my New Year's ritual—a way of sharing grace with the people I love.

My friend Terry created a unique spiritual experience for guests at his son's Bar Mitzvah. Terry wanted to acknowledge the rite of passage into manhood by introducing Alexander to six distinctly different male friends who would each take him on an adventure to teach him something about becoming a man. Alexander experienced everything from a raucous poker game, to a photo shoot with a well-established designer, to a day at the Museum of Fine Arts with an artist, where the two of them sketched all day long. During the Bar Mitzvah ceremony, each man had an opportunity to talk about the special qualities he witnessed in Alexander during their time together. Then Alexander shared the lessons he learned about manhood from each of the six men.

The service was beautiful. The love and admiration the

men expressed for Alexander, and the knowledge that Alexander gleaned from his adventures, taught us all something important about life, relationships, and the unique perspective we have to share with one another. After the ceremony, it was obvious that the intimacy created by this special service had affected everyone. Strangers introduced themselves to each other and sat down to discuss their own thoughts about entering adulthood. During my conversations with several people I hadn't known before, I noticed that our discussions started out on a much deeper level than what typically occurs between strangers. Terry and his son Alexander had done a fine job of creating a memory that raised the spiritual consciousness of everyone who attended this beautiful event.

THE GIFT OF TOUGH LOVE

Sometimes what we don't do or say can be a gift of grace. Our willingness to step back and get out of the way sets in motion the chance for the Divine to work miracles in another person's life. That's exactly what happened to my client Rochelle and her brother Tim. By the time Rochelle realized that her brother had a serious drinking problem, she had already bailed Tim out of jail once, lent him money to feed his family, and helped him to get a new job. By doing these things for Tim, Rochelle honestly thought she was helping him get his life on track. But instead, it only made things worse.

One day, while discussing the situation with a coworker it was suggested that Rochelle attend an AA meeting to hear about how others became sober. Rochelle was unfamiliar with AA but was open to the idea that it might shed some light on the problem. After attending meetings for three months she began to see that her good intentions were actually contributing to Tim's problem. To become a spiritual change agent for Tim, Rochelle would need to stop cleaning up his messes, giving him money, and being a peacemaker with his wife and kids. As a result, Tim would have to be accountable for his actions.

At first Rochelle admitted that the advice she kept getting from recovering alcoholics was contrary to what she felt was compassionate and loving. She cared deeply for her brother and hated to see him and his family suffer. But, as she acquired the courage and knowledge to address this delicate matter, she agreed to give tough love a try. Then, whenever her brother called for money or some type of help, Rochelle simply said, "I love you and I can't do that for you anymore. There is a place where you can get the help you need and it's called AA. If and when you decide to go, I'll be right there by your side."

Several months later Tim's situation was even worse. His wife was threatening to leave him, there was a good chance that he would lose his kids, and he had been put on notice with his job. During this period of time, Tim called Rochelle nearly every day asking for help and guidance. As painful as it was to say no, she stuck by her line, "I love you and I can't do that for you anymore. There is a place where you can get the help you need and it's called AA. If and when you decide to go, I'll be happy to come along."

Finally, one morning, hung over and embarrassed by his

behavior at a bar, Tim called Rochelle and admitted that he needed help. He agreed to attend one meeting. Fortunately for them both, one meeting turned into two, and after a few false starts (with Rochelle sticking to her tough love plan), Tim got into recovery once and for all.

While it was too late for his marriage (his wife had had enough and decided that she couldn't trust his sobriety), Tim's recovery brought him and his sister closer. With six months of sobriety under his belt, Tim thanked Rochelle for her willingness to stand firm. He admitted, "As painful as it was to hear you tell me that you couldn't give me what I wanted, it was exactly what I needed to hear. Your honesty may have saved my life."

WHEN GRACE IS A LONG-TERM ASSIGNMENT

My friend Karla shared another example of how we can give a gift of grace to someone in need. Karla's spouse Adam suffered from depression. For more than two years he had been in and out of doctors' offices desperately trying to get a handle on his problem. He had been unemployed for eleven months and most nights when Karla came home from work, she'd find him in front of the television, watching movies with a hollow, vacant look in his eyes.

Karla admitted that she felt mentally and physically exhausted from the stress caused by Adam's depression, her busy job, and all of her household responsibilities. "There were some nights," she admitted, "when I'd drive home from work crying and praying, 'Please God don't let him be rolled up in a ball on the couch tonight. Let him be okay just this once.' Then I'd walk through the door and sure enough he'd be there on the couch and I'd need to pull myself together to be there for him once again. But as hard as it was during this difficult time, I knew Adam needed a safe place to heal. I didn't shame, judge, or nag him and in the process learned that being a source of grace for someone is not always a short-term assignment."

It took two years for Adam to find a treatment protocol that worked. When I asked Karla how she found the determination and energy to hang in there for so long, she said, "Along with the support of a few loving friends, I remember finding a picture of Mother Teresa. I could see the weight of other people's pain in the deep wrinkles of her face or the way she walked slightly stooped over. She was such an amazing woman who cared deeply for others. When I felt especially tired or down, I would pull out her picture. Believe it or not, I was able to draw strength from what I saw in her eyes. When I think about it, I guess Mother Teresa was my source of grace."

Karla's story is an inspiring example of how we can go far beyond what we think we're capable of to support another human being. Sometimes it's easier to handle the ups and downs of supporting someone through a difficult time when we see it as a spiritual practice. This means that while we take good care of ourselves, getting support, and scheduling downtime, we also become a steward for the care of someone else's soul while they heal. When I meet people who walk side-by-side with loved ones as they face grief, aging, or long-term illness, I am humbled by the strength of the human spirit.

CREATING AN ONGOING CIRCLE OF GRACE

While having dinner with my uncle Lenny, I asked him about his thoughts on grace. "Grace is one of my favorite topics," he replied. "Each day I say a little prayer asking God to allow me to touch at least one person by saying or doing something that helps in some way. It never fails. I always seem to get an opportunity."

Lenny works at a health club. One day, while talking with a guest, he heard a story that inspired him to share the gift of grace with others in a tangible way. The guest was a Christian gentleman who told Lenny a story about a medal he received during a time when his son was very ill. Then he reached into his pocket, pulled out a small object with an imprint of the Blessed Virgin Mary on it, and explained, "Several years ago, as I faced the possibility that I might lose my son, a man gave me this medal. He told me that there were a group of people praying for any person who had it in his or her possession. He placed it in my hand and informed me that my son and I were now recipients of this weekly gift. His kind gesture went right to my heart. It felt comforting to know that we were receiving that kind of support during such a painful time in our lives. Ever since that day I make sure I have a medal in my pocket and when I come across someone in need, I retell the story and give one away." With that, he reached into his pocket, pulled out a medal, and handed it to Lenny. "Give this to someone in need and when you do, I'll replace it with another."

The medal, called a Miraculous Medal, owes its origin to Catherine Labouré, a member of the Daughters of Charity of St. Vincent de Paul who later became known as Sister Catherine. In 1830 the Blessed Virgin Mary appeared to her on three separate occasions. During the second appearance, Sister Catherine reported that the Blessed Virgin appeared as if standing on a globe, holding a golden ball in her hands that represented the world. There were rings on her fingers set with gems, some of which emitted rays of light. "These," Sister Catherine said, "were the symbols of graces which would be bestowed on all who asked for them." Sister Catherine then went on to report that the Blessed Virgin said, "The gems from which rays do not fall are the graces for which souls forget to ask." Staring at the vision before her, Sister Catherine heard the voice of the Blessed Virgin say, "Have a medal struck after this model. All who wear it will receive great graces; they should wear it around their neck. Graces will abound for those who wear it with confidence."

When Sister Catherine's body was exhumed for beatification in 1933, it was found to be fully intact, as fresh as the day it was buried. She was canonized in 1947.

Lenny was so inspired by this man's story (and his gift) that he couldn't wait to give the medal away. He knew it wouldn't be long before he'd have a chance. He soon did and since then, has continued to give away medals. "The response has been amazing," Lenny said. "I recently gave a medal to a big, burly guy whose brother was dying of cancer. This man had lost his father to the same disease several years before. He wasn't a religious man so I was hesitant at first, but I decided to give it to him anyway." Lenny said that the moment he put the medal in the man's hand and informed him that he and his brother were now the recipients of weekly prayers, the man broke down and started to cry. "I've learned that the religion or spiritual orientation of a person doesn't matter when you give the gift of prayer. I've never had anyone turn me down."

Whether it's religious inspiration or the gift of hope, Lenny says that the medal offers people comfort and reminds them that they are not alone. "Each time I hand a medal to someone, I see his or her eyes light up, and I feel like I've done my small part to spread a little grace around the world." He certainly does. Lenny has created an ongoing circle of grace.

At a time when there is so much pain and suffering in the world, it's comforting to know that there are people who are committed to being a source of light in the midst of darkness. We need the healing power of grace now more than ever.

———◆———

As we come to the end of our journey, it is my hope that this book provides some reassurance that there really is a powerful guiding force available to each and every one of us. I believe that opening our hearts to this force and staying connected to our innate Divinity gives us our greatest chance to survive and thrive in a complex and challenging world. If the "coincidences" that occurred that night in Dallas are indicative of what happens when we bring grace into our work and our conversations with others, it is critical that we do so.

As I complete this chapter of my life, I know that it's just one stop on a long road to spiritual wholeness—an adventure that we all share together. There will be days when we question our faith, forget to surrender our will, or wonder whether God really exists at all. It's during these times that we need to reach out to one another as fellow spiritual pioneers, so we can be reminded of how a Higher Power supports us all.

As you continue on your journey, may the light of grace illuminate your path and may you always feel a solid connection to the Divine Source that creates and sustains us all.

Experiment: Become a Spiritual Pioneer

The final experiment has two parts—one that supports your spiritual growth, and one that supports others.

PART 1—BUILD A SPIRITUAL COMMUNITY

As you continue on this journey, you'll want to surround yourself with an intentional community of people who support your commitment to consciousness. Just like in the beginning, when you made a choice to wake up, you'll continue to need like-minded people around you to encourage your growth. It's easy for us to feel lonely or unsure of ourselves as we chart a new course. Spiritual pioneers need comrades to keep them focused and strong.

Create a spiritual community. For example, you might start a dialogue group and invite people from all faiths and traditions to come together on a regular basis to share their beliefs and spiritual practices in a safe and open format. Not only will this allow people to become more knowledgeable about other spiritual practices, it will teach tolerance and respect for the beliefs of others.

If you're already a member of a church, temple, or synagogue, get more involved. Serve on a committee, lead a fund-raising effort, or create a program that supports fellow members. You might start a weekly prayer group, a book study group, or some kind of youth program that brings together adults and teenagers.

PART 2—EXPAND YOUR CIRCLE OF GRACE

Tikun-olam is a Hebrew concept meaning "Improve the world," and part two of this experiment is designed to support you in taking a more proactive role as a spiritual pioneer so you can do just that.

Start with small acts of kindness. Borrowing from my uncle's story, you might start each day with your own prayer:

> *Dear God, please allow me to touch at least one person today.*

Then, make it a practice to look for one small thing you can do each day to share the gift of grace with a fellow human being. You might:

- Smile at a stranger.
- Take an elderly person to the grocery store.
- Send an anonymous note to someone acknowledging his or her unique gift or talent.
- Purchase a dozen roses and give one each to a coworker, neighbor, post office clerk, and so on.
- Unasked, run an errand for someone.
- Bring an unexpected gift to someone who could use a message of love.

If you'd like to give to others on a larger scale, you could:

• Adopt a family in your community and send an anonymous gift once a month.
• Spend some time each week with a lonely child.
• Talk to and listen to an older person (with emphasis on the listen to part).
• Become involved with a literacy volunteer group and explore a variety of spiritual books.
• Start a meditation group in your workplace.
• Start a not-for-profit organization that raises money for a needy cause.

By investing your time and energy in a specific project, you not only give yourself a chance to make your spiritual values a more tangible part of your life, but you also build strong, intimate bonds with others. These relationships will have a direct influence on generations to come.

Resources

BOOKS

Balancing Heaven and Earth: A Memoir of Visions, Dreams, and Realizations by Robert Johnson (Harper San Francisco, 1998)

> *One of my favorites books, it's an inspiring memoir and personal guide to Johnson's concept of self-realization. This book shares many fascinating stories of Johnson's life and his spiritual evolution.*

A Book of Angels by Sophy Burnham (Wellspring/Ballantine, 1990)

> *This book tells the extraordinary stories of present-day encounters with angels, traces the appearance of angels in*

various cultures, and explores how writers—such as Dante, Milton, and Shakespeare—have responded to angels throughout history.

The Book of Mystical Chapters translated by John Anthony McGuckin (Shambhala Publications, 2003)

This book contains meditations from the desert fathers and other early Christian contemplatives.

Loving Through Heartsongs by Matti J. T. Stepanek (VSP Books/Hyperion Press, 2003)

A beautiful and moving book containing a collection of inspirational poems written by this wise and loving young man.

The Purpose Driven Life: What on Earth Am I Here For? by Rich Warren (Zondervan, 2002)

This book is said to be a blueprint for Christian living, taking readers on a 40-day spiritual journey to answer the question: What on earth am I here for?

Sacred Fireplace: Life and Teachings of a Lakota Medicine Man by Pete S. Catches, Sr. (Clear Light Publishers, 1999)

A wonderfully written account of Oglala Lakotans' culture and spiritual beliefs.

White Fire: A Portrait of Women Spiritual Leaders in America by Malka Drucker with photographs by Gay Block (Skylight Paths Publishing, 2003)

This book gives voice and image to the often overlooked narrative of women's spiritual leadership in America today.

Who Dies? An Investigation of Conscious Living and Conscious Dying by Stephen Levine and Ondrea Levine (Anchor, 1989)

This book shows how to open oneself to the immensity of death with compassion and calmness.

WEBSITES

www.tikun-olam.net

This website is dedicated to finding Jewish ways in which to improve the world.

HOW TO USE THIS BOOK

Here are three ways to use this book:

1. When you find yourself questioning the existence of grace, close your eyes, take a deep breath, and ask to be taken to a page that will provide you with insight. Then open the book to a random page.

2. Invite a small group of friends to your home and ask each person to bring their favorite passage from the book along with a personal story that relates to the topic. You might also ask each guest to bring a sacred object for a gift exchange.

3. Form a book group with others who are interested in learning to improve their ability to see the signs of grace. Schedule a monthly meeting and assign a chapter to read beforehand. Have each member conduct the experiment at the end of the chapter so they can come prepared to share their results. For further inspiration between meetings, take note of how grace has touched your lives so you can share examples with each other.

Here are some questions that can be used for group discussion:

- How has the power of grace already influenced your life?
- When did you experience a moment of truth? What happened?
- What tools have been most helpful to you on your spiritual journey?
- What evidence of grace have you uncovered from your past?
- Who are the significant spiritual change agents in your life?
- When were you faced with a situation that forced you to surrender? What happened?
- How has your life changed as a result of conducting the experiments in the book?
- Will you share one example of how you've been a conduit of grace for others?

To find group members, feel free to visit the Life Makeover Group section of our website at www.cherylrichardson.com.

ABOUT THE AUTHOR

Cheryl Richardson is the author of the *New York Times* best-selling books *Take Time for Your Life, Life Makeovers,* and *Stand Up for Your Life.* Her work has been covered widely in the media including *The Today Show, Good Morning America, CBS This Morning, New York Times, Good Housekeeping,* and *O Magazine.* Cheryl led the Lifestyle Makeover Series on *The Oprah Winfrey Show* and accompanied Ms. Winfrey on the "Live Your Best Life" nationwide tour.

For more information on Cheryl's retreats, to find a Life Makeover Group near you, or to receive her free weekly e-newsletter, visit www.cherylrichardson.com.